Maximizing Employee Retention Credits

Maximizing Employee Retention Credits

How to Qualify for, Claim and Collect Bigger Employee Retention Credits

By
Stephen L. Nelson, CPA

Copyright © 2021 Stephen L. Nelson. All rights reserved.

ISBN: 9798455450525

Published by Percheron Hill LLC
5387 242nd PL NE
Redmond, WA 98053
http://www.percheronhill.com

This book shares information about the employee retention credit created by Section 2301 of the Coronavirus Aid, Relief, and Economic Security Act (CARES Act) and by Section 3134 of the Families First Coronavirus Response Act (Families First Act).

The book is not intended to replace the services of a competent legal, tax, or business advisor. If legal or other expert assistance is required, the services of a professional should be sought.

While both the publisher and author have made every effort to offer the most current, correct, and clearly expressed information possible, inadvertent errors can occur and the rules and regulations governing accounting standards and tax laws often change. Further, the application and impact of rules and laws can vary widely from case to case based upon the unique facts involved. Be careful!

Acknowledgements

I want to thank Dan Chodan, Ed Zollars and Tony Nitti for the ways that their writing, teaching and Twitter messages helped educate me and clarify my thinking on the employee retention credits.

I also want to thank my work colleagues Christian Block and Elsa Zhu for their review and useful criticism of the manuscript.

Any errors or confusion the pages of this book still show are solely my responsibility. But fewer errors and less confusion appears here as a result of the help these experts provided.

About the Author

A CPA for over three decades, and the managing member of Nelson CPA PLLC, Stephen L. Nelson holds an MBA in Finance from the University of Washington and an MS in Taxation from Golden Gate University.

He is the author of dozens of best-selling books about accounting and finance, including *Quicken for Dummies* and *QuickBooks for Dummies* (which each sold more than 1,000,000 copies) and the author of the tax monograph, *Maximizing Section 199A Deductions*.

He also taught the "Choice of Entity: S Corporation vs Limited Liability Company" class in the graduate tax school at Golden Gate University.

Table of Contents

Introduction 9
    Four Things to Understand as You Start 10
    Why This Book 11
    How to Read this Book...12
    What This Book Covers..12
Chapter 1: ERC Formulas in a Nutshell........................16
    What is an Employee Retention Credit.................16
    Six Basic Employee Retention Credit Rules 17
    Collecting the ERC Refund.....................................20
Chapter 2: Eligible Employers..22
    Substantial Decline in Gross Receipts Eligibility...22
        Substantial Decline Eligibility in 2020...............23
        Substantial Decline Eligibility in 2021...............23
        Taxable Organization Gross Receipts 24
        Tax-exempt Organization Gross Receipts 25
        PPP Forgiveness as Gross Receipts 26
        When Employer Can't Compare to 2019..........26
        Alternative Quarter Comparison.......................27
    Full Suspension Eligibility 29
    Partial Suspension Eligibility 32
        More than Nominal Standard 33
        Multiple Jurisdictions..34
    Recovery Start-up Business 37
        How Recovery Startup Business ERC Works ..37
        Recovery Startup Business Credit Limit...........40

Chapter 3: Qualified Wages 41
Wages in General 41
Qualified Wages in 2020 42
Employers with more than 100 Employees   42
Employers with 100 or Fewer Employees 46
Allocable Qualified Health Plan Expenses 47
Qualified Wages in 2021 48
Large Eligible Employer Definition Change 48
No 30-day Lookback for Large Employer 49
Severely Financially Distressed Employer 49
Qualified Wages Intervals 50
Disqualified Wages 52
Wages and Health Insurance Paid with PPP Funds 52
Reduction in Qualified Wages from Other Credits 53
Owner and Owner Family Member Wages 54

Chapter 4: Start-up Trades or Businesses 58
ERC Trade or Business Definition 58
The Section 162 Trade or Business Meaning 60
When a Start-up Business Actually Starts 62
Starting a Second Trade or Business 63
Gross Receipts Allowed in Three Preceding Tax Years 63
Qualified Wages May Be Incurred Prior to Starting 63
Statutory and Regulatory Language 64
New Trade or Business Planning Tips 65
Show Something is Starting 65

    Explicitly Document the Timing Works 67
    Clearly Separating New Trade or Business 68
  Avoiding Hobby Taint 70
Chapter 5: How Aggregation Works 72
  Where Aggregation Matters 72
  When Employers Get Aggregated 75
    Section 52 Controlled Group of Corporation ... 75
    Section 414(m) Affiliated Service Group 77
  Tribes and Tribal Entities 77
  When Employer Acquires a Trade or Business 78
Chapter 6: Balancing ERC and PPP 81
  Review of the PPP Loan Formula 82
  Review of the PPP Forgiveness Formula 82
  General Rule Regarding PPP Payroll 83
  Exception to the General Payroll Rule 85
  The PPP Nonpayroll Costs 86
    Mortgage Interest Costs 87
    Rent Costs 89
    Self-Rental Costs 91
    Utilities Costs 92
    Home Office Expenses 94
    Operations Expenditures 94
    Property Damage Costs 95
    Supplier Costs 95
    Worker Protection Expenditures 95
  Two Tactics to Optimize PPP and ERC 98
  IRS Guidance on PPP Wages 99
  PPP Forgiveness vs ERC 104
Chapter 7: Tax Accounting for ERC Transactions 106
  The Basic Rule: Adjust Deductions for Credits 106
  Mismatched Deductions and Credits 107
  Example ERC Bookkeeping Transactions 107

  When Amending 941 Return..................................108
  When Refund on Original 941............................109
Chapter 8: Tips for Maximizing ERC Refunds..................**110**
 Tip #1: Use Eligibility Based on Gross Receipts.....110
 Tip #2: Look at 2020 If Employer Started in 2019 .111
 Tip #3: Consider the Alternative Quarter Method..111
 Tip #4: Expand the Interval of Eligibility................112
 Tip #5: Verify Your Local Non-profit Knows.........112
 Tip #6: Acquire Another Trade or Business...........112
 Tip #7: Use Nonpayroll Costs for PPP Forgiveness 113
 Tip #8: Maximize Owner and Family Wages.........114
 Tip #9: Use a 24-week Covered Period....................114
 Tip #10: Start a Recovery Start-up Business 114
 Tip #11: Start a New Trade or Business ASAP.......115
Glossary of Terms...**117**
Appendix A: Section 2301 ....**121**
Appendix B: Sections 206, 207 and 303 ....**130**
Appendix C: Section 3134..**151**

Introduction

In the spring of 2020, as the COVID-19 pandemic roared into the world's consciousness, the United States Congress did something extraordinary. They began giving away money—so essentially free money—to taxpayers, businesses, and non-profit organizations damaged by the pandemic.

Many varieties of this financial support appeared. Extended unemployment benefits. Paycheck Protection Program loans. Targeted financial support for state and local governments. And for some industries, like the airlines.

This book talks about one of the less-popular forms of financial support that Congress created, the employee retention credit.

The employment retention credit never gained as much attention or popularity as other support programs, such as the Paycheck Projection Program.[1] But you don't want to let the unpopularity of the credit influence you.

The employee retention credit, as compared to any other existing federal financial support, merits close examination. And for three reasons.

---

[1] Our CPA firm actively published articles at our firm blog to help small businesses benefit from both the Paycheck Protection Program (PPP) and the Employee Retention Credit (ERC). Reader interest and traffic for the PPP tended to run ten times the interest and traffic for the ERC.

First, the size of the employee retention credits subsidy easily approaches and, in many cases, exceeds the size of the Paycheck Protection Program loans employers received. An employer who received a $50,000 PPP loan, for example, may qualify for $100,000 of employee retention credits. An employer who qualified for a $250,000 PPP loan may qualify for $400,000 or $500,000 of employee retention credits.

A second reason to closely look at employee retention credits? The credits still exist as a form of support. If you missed applying for a PPP loan last year, for example, you missed your chance. That ship sailed, so to speak.

In comparison, if you didn't apply for an employee retention credit last year but you qualified? Sure, you're late. But you can still retroactively apply. Now.

Finally, a third important reason. New businesses may more easily get financial support using the employee retention credit. In fact, depending on when you're reading this book (which I'm writing during the summer of 2021) you may still be able to get employee retention credits for a trade or business you have not even yet started.

Four Things to Understand as You Start

You want to understand four things as you start your reading.

First, an employer gets the employee retention credit for paying wages to employees. And more specifically, for paying wages to non-owner and non-family-member employees. You typically won't get an employee retention credit, or ERC, for paying a shareholder-employee. Or for paying a relative of the owner.

Second, the ERC formulas provide the biggest subsidies for middle-income and lower-income workers. The formula for 2020 may pay half of the wages a part-time or seasonal worker earns. The formula for 2021 may pay seventy percent of the wages a middle-income or lower-income worker earns.

Third, the ERC laws favor small employers. You'll see this as you read through the coming chapters. Furthermore, the employee retention credit laws provide extraordinary support to the smallest firms. The skewing of benefits toward the smallest employers means that these firms should look closely at how to qualify for, claim, and maximize ERCs.

A fourth thing to note—and somewhat contrary to the point just made: The ERC laws burden employers and their accountants with surprising complexity. Determining when you qualify? Sometimes tricky. Especially in borderline cases. Calculating the precise credits? Well, you'll need a spreadsheet. Let's admit that up front. Finally, optimizing your situation so you get a larger credit? You'll have to know the law's gritty details.

Why This Book

This book exists for two groups of readers.

First, for the businesses and non-profit organizations impacted by the COVID-19 pandemic. Hopefully, this book helps you learn about, qualify for, and then claim the largest possible employee retention credits.

Second, if you're a bookkeeper or accountant, maybe an attorney, the book exists so you can understand how these credits work. And so you can help clients maximize the ERC benefits they receive.

How to Read this Book

You don't have to read this book from start to finish. A reader may just use it as a reference.

But for the record, a business owner, bookkeeper, accountant, or attorney should be able to sit down and in *roughly two or three hou*rs learn most of the complex details, risks, and opportunities related to employee retention credits, including how to qualify, maximize, and claim the refunds.

I'd like to think that in a few hours, you'll not only know if you can get $50,000 or maybe even $500,000 of ERC refunds. I would hope you know what you need to do to get those refunds. And how quickly you need to act.

What This Book Covers

The chapter list follows:

Chapter 1, "The ERC Formulas in a Nutshell," explains how the employee retention credit formulas work.

Chapter 2, "Eligible Employers," explains which employers qualify for ERCs. Millions of firms qualify, which in a sense is a tragedy. Qualification means a firm or organization got beat up by the COVID-19 pandemic. But if a silver lining to this storm cloud exists? That silver lining is your firm very probably qualifies. For at least some credits.

Chapter 3, "Qualified Wages and Health Benefits," describes which wages and health care benefits plug into the formulas that calculate the ERC refunds.

Chapter 4, "Startup Trades or Businesses," describes how the ERC works for new businesses. This feature of the ERC laws—support for brand new businesses—is something business owners and their advisors need to act on immediately.

Chapter 5, "How Aggregation Works," explains when and how a business owner needs to aggregate businesses. If you own and operate several different businesses, the ERC laws probably combine, or aggregate, those businesses for purposes of the ERC.

Chapter 6, "Balancing ERC and PPP," explains how the PPP forgiveness application process impacts your ERC calculations. And how to apply for PPP forgiveness in a manner which protects ETC claims.

Chapter 7, "Tax Accounting for ERC Transactions," quickly steps a reader through the tax accounting rules for ERC transactions.

Finally, Chapter 8, "Tips and Tricks," points out steps that employers may take to simplify applying for ERC refunds and to maximize credits. In effect, Chapter 8 summarizes the important bits of the preceding chapters.

The book includes a glossary, which readers who are not tax accountants may want to dogear now and then refer to as they read through the chapters.

Finally, the book includes three appendices, too.

Appendix A provides a copy of the original employee retention credit statute, Section 2301 Employee Retention Credit for Employers Subject to Closure Due to COVID-19.

Appendix B provides copies of Sections 206, 207 and 303 of the Consolidated Appropriations Act (2021) because these change the employee retention credit formulas and rules for 2021.

Appendix C provides a copy of the updated employee retention credit that applies to credits for the last half of 2021, Section 3134 Employee Retention Credit for Employers Subject to Closure Due to COVID-19.

The book includes these appendices because some readers will struggle to find the right, updated copy of the statutes. Also, some readers may want to refer to the statutes as they read. (Footnotes often point to the statutes.)

And this tip: Readers may want to download the following IRS Notices and then either save them to a computer or print hardcopies:
- IRS Notice 2021-20: Guidance on the Employee Retention Credit under Section 2301 of the Coronavirus Aid, Relief, and Economic Security Act (102 pages)
- IRS Notice 2021-23: Guidance on the Employee Retention Credit under the CARES Act for the First and Second Calendar Quarters of 2021 (17 pages)

- IRS Notice 2021-49: Guidance on the Employee Retention Credit under Section 3134 of the Code and on Miscellaneous Issues Related to the Employee Retention Credit (34 pages)

These documents should be available in the IRS's online drop box, which is available here:

https://www.irs.gov/downloads/irs-drop

Two other things to mention. First, to let readers move through this material faster, most citations, technical details and then anything tangential appear in the footnotes. So, look there if you need more information. (As a guess? Business owners and managers may often want to skip looking at the footnotes. And professionals helping their clients with ERCs may often want to read them.)

A second thing: The employee retention credit program itself may evolve. New legislation in process proposes additional changes. What's more, though the ERC will only provide subsidies through the end of 2021, surely the Internal Revenue Service will provide additional guidance over the coming months.

To deal with these changes, our CPA blog, **http://evergreensmallbusiness.com**, will provide additional coverage of these developments. And you may want to refer there if you need more information.

And now let's dig into the details.

Chapter 1: ERC Formulas in a Nutshell

This chapter provides a quick overview of how the employee retention credit works by looking at the formulas.

If you already understand well the arithmetic of employee retention credits, you may want to skip ahead to the next chapters, which talk about eligible employers, qualified wages and aggregation rules.

Many readers, however, probably benefit from a quick review of how the ERC formulas work.

What is an Employee Retention Credit?

Employee retention credits reward an employer by paying a large chunk of the employee's wages.

In 2020, for example, the federal government will pay an employer up to a $5,000 credit for wages paid and group health insurance provided to each employee in 2020.[2]

In 2021, the deal gets even better. The federal government will pay up to a $28,000 credit for wages paid and group health insurance provided to each employee in 2021.[3]

---

[2] The $5,000 per employee per year credit represents the original ERC formula created by the "Coronavirus Aid, Relief, and Economic Security Act", or "CARES Act." The CARES Act was passed by Congress on March 25, 2020 and signed into law on March 27, 2020.

[3] The $7,000 per employee per quarter credit represents the revised ERC formula

> *Example 1.* A small business employs two workers who each earn $40,000 annually and it qualifies for full employee retention credits for both 2020 and 2021. In 2020, the firm receives $10,000 of credits ($5,000 for each employee). In 2021, the firm receives $56,000 of credits ($28,000 for each employee).

The credit formula, by the way, works differently in 2020 and 2021.

In 2020, the employee retention credit formula equals fifty percent of the wages and group health insurance paid but not more than $5,000 per employee for the year. (The 2020 credit formula, then, looks only at the first $10,000 of wages and group health insurance paid for the year.)[4]

In 2021, the employee retention credit formula equals seventy percent of the wages and group health insurance paid but not more than $7,000 per employee per quarter. (The 2021 credit formula looks at the first $10,000 of wages and group health insurance paid during each quarter.)

Six Basic Employee Retention Credit Rules

Six basic rules apply to the employee retention credit.

The first rule? The credit works, potentially, for wages and group health insurance paid after March 12, 2020 and through December 31, 2021.[5]

---

created by the "Consolidated Appropriations Act (2021)." The Consolidated Appropriations Act (2021) was passed by Congress on December 21, 2020 and signed into law on December 27, 2020.

[4] Section 2301(a) and Section 2301(b)(1), as reproduced in Appendix A

[5] Congress is discussing ending some eligibility for ERCs before the end of 2021 as this book goes to press. One bipartisan infrastructure bill that appeared in early

> *Example 2.* A small business employs paid employees the first quarter of 2020. Wages paid after March 12 potentially count for ERC refunds.

The second rule: A firm potentially becomes eligible for the credit in any of three ways: If its operations were suspended by government order, if it experienced a significant contraction in quarterly revenues typically as compared to 2019, and if it started a new trade or business. (Chapter 2 talks more about all three qualification methods. And Chapter 4 talks about qualifying by starting a new trade or business.)

A third rule says that you can't "double dip" and thereby get a credit and refund if some other federal government program already provided you money to pay the wages. For example, you don't get employee retention credits for wages you paid using Paycheck Protection Program funds. Or if you received other payroll tax credits that, in effect, funded employee wages.[6]

The fourth rule? Large eligible employers typically only take the credit only on wages paid to employees for not working. For 2020 employee retention credits, a large eligible employer is a firm employing more than 100 full-time employees in 2019. For 2021 employee retention credits, a large eligible employer is a firm employing more than 500 full-time employees in 2019.

August, for example, proposes that the ERC only apply to new or trade or business situations, or "Recovery Startup Businesses," which Chapters 2 and 4 discuss.

[6] The original version of the employer retention credit statute, included as Appendix A, said an employer could not receive both a Paycheck Protection Program loan and employee retention credits. As the COVID-19 pandemic worsened over time, Congress changed that rule and said employers could tap both forms of government assistance. The one logical rule: You could not use Paycheck Protection Program money to pay, for example, wages during the third quarter. And then calculate employee retention credits for those same wages.

> *Example 3.* A large eligible-for-ERC firm employed more than 500 full-time workers in 2019. In 2020, it furloughed but continued to pay 20 of these workers. Because the firm is a large eligible employer only the wages for the 20 furloughed employees count in the ERC calculations. In 2020, that might mean the firm receives $100,000 of credits for the year ($5,000 for each of the 20 employees). In 2021, the firm receives $140,000 for each quarter it's eligible ($7,000 for each of the 20 employees.)

For small eligible employers, in comparison, the employer takes the full credit, potentially, on all their workers' wages (subject to the third rule just mentioned).

> *Example 4.* A small eligible employer with 100 full-time workers also qualifies for ERC and again furloughs ten percent, or 10, of the workers. Because the employer employs 100 or fewer full-time employees, the ERC formula looks at the wages paid to all 100 employees. In 2020, the firm receives $500,000 of credits for the year ($5,000 for each employee). In 2021, the firm receives $700,000 of credits for each quarter the firm is eligible ($7,000 for each employee).

The fifth rule: A business owner aggregates the businesses she or he or they own. For example, if you own a restaurant (maybe operated as a sole proprietorship), 100 percent of a consulting business (maybe operated as an S corporation), and a majority interest in a partnership, you aggregate all of these businesses to determine if you are a large or small employer, whether your operations qualify (according to the second rule mentioned earlier), what the wages total and so forth.

And, finally, a sixth rule: While the statutes say that the employee retention is available to eligible employers operating a trade or business, the Treasury Department and the IRS define "trade or business" very broadly here. The employee retention credit may be used by tax-exempt organizations organized under Section 501(c) of the Internal Revenue Code and by tribal governments and tribal entities.

This book won't focus much on these two special-case situations. But if you work in or for an organization that falls into either category, know that the ERC may be able to help that organization too.

Collecting the ERC Refund

As noted earlier, an employer makes the ERC refund claim on its quarterly 941 payroll tax return.

The IRS notices that provide guidance to employers tell them to report the employee retention credit as a reduction in their payroll tax deposit liabilities. This method should mean that an eligible employer immediately sees a positive cash flow impact.

> *Example 5.* An eligible employer realizes it qualifies for a $50,000 employee retention credit. It had planned to make a $25,000 payroll tax deposit for each of its next two payrolls. It can skip making those deposits. The $50,000 in effect "pays" both of the next two payroll's deposits.

Small eligible employers may also request an advance refund using Form 7200.

Finally, if an employer failed to include an employee retention credit on a quarterly tax return, the employer can amend that quarter's tax return, show the employee retention credit, and then claim a refund.

One wrinkle: The IRS instructs employers to claim ERC on wages for the first quarter of 2020 on the second quarter's 941. In other words, qualified wages paid after March 12, 2020 and before April 1, 2020 produce an ERC for the second quarter's 941 return.[7]

If you should have claimed an ERC refund on a 2020 941 payroll return but did not? You need to go back and amend the original tax return using the 941-X payroll return.

Three other comments about this. First, when an employer faces a simple ERC calculation—especially one for the current quarter—an outside payroll tax service may be able to just "add" the ERC amounts to the 941 return they prepare.

If your business should get an ERC for this current quarter, for example, you may be able to just "tell" the payroll service that your business qualifies.

Second, in more complex situations and when amending previously filed 941 returns, employers may need to consult their tax accountants.

Third, finally, as we write this it appears that employers face long-processing times for their refund claims. At least weeks and possibly months, according to what we hear from other tax accountants.

---

[7] The IRS issued this instruction in an online FAQ. The short instruction simply asks and answers a question saying, "How does an Eligible Employer report qualified wages paid in the first quarter of 2020? An Eligible Employer that pays qualified wages in the first quarter of 2020 should report those wages on Form 941, Employer's Quarterly Federal Tax Return, for the second quarter of 2020.

Chapter 2: Eligible Employers

An employer becomes eligible for employee retention credits in one of four ways:
- Suffering a substantial decline in gross receipts (usually as compared to 2019),
- Full suspending of operations as a result of a government order,
- Partial suspending of more than a nominal part of operations as a result of a government order, or
- Starting up a new trade or business.

The paragraphs that follow describe each of these eligibility methods in detail.

Substantial Decline in Gross Receipts Eligibility

An employer who continues to operate a business during 2020 and 2021 but who experiences a substantial decline in gross receipts qualifies for ERC.

The definition of "substantial," however, varies by year.

Substantial Decline Eligibility in 2020

For 2020, an employer gains eligibility when it suffers a greater than a fifty reduction in gross receipts in some quarter of 2020.[8] An employer's eligibility ends either January 1, 2021 or the calendar quarter following the first 2020 calendar quarter in which an employer's quarterly gross receipts exceed 80 percent of its gross receipts for the same calendar quarter in 2019.[9]

> *Example 6.* A small eligible employer generates $100,000 in quarterly gross receipts for each quarter of 2019. In the second quarter of 2020, gross receipts decline to $40,000. That decline creates eligibility for the ERC. If the small business's gross receipts rise to $80,000 in the second quarter, it maintains its ERC eligibility for the second quarter and for the third quarter. If for the third quarter, the firm gross receipts rise to $81,000, the firm loses its ERC eligibility for the fourth quarter.

Substantial Decline Eligibility in 2021

For 2021, eligibility requires a greater than twenty percent reduction in gross receipts as compared to the same quarter of 2019.[10] Note that the determination of eligibility for a quarter in 2021, then, is made separately for each quarter, based on that threshold.

---

[8] Sec, 2301(c)(2)(B), as reproduced in Appendix A.

[9] IRS Notice 2021-23

[10] Section 2301(c)(2)(A)(ii)(II) of the CARES Act, as amended by section 207(d)(1)(A) of the Relief Act.

> *Example 7.* If an employer generated $1,000,000 of gross receipts in each quarter of 2019 but for the first quarter of 2021 generated $790,000 of gross receipts, it qualifies for ERC. If in the second quarter, it generates $800,000 of gross receipts—so exactly 80 percent of the 2019 quarterly number—it fails to qualify for ERC for the second quarter. Under current law, if for the third quarter it generates $790,000 of gross receipts, the firm again gains eligibility for ERC for that quarter.

Taxable Organization Gross Receipts

The employee retention credit statutes define gross receipts by referencing Internal Revenue Code Section 448(c) which in turn defines "gross receipts" in the companion regulations.[11]

Essentially, a taxpayer uses the same accounting method as used on their tax returns and includes all the income shown there.

If the business tax return uses the accrual method of accounting, for example, an employer uses the accrual method of accounting to determine its gross receipts. If the business tax return uses the cash method of accounting, alternatively, an employer uses the cash method of accounting to determine its gross receipts.

Gross receipts get adjusted down for returns and allowances and up for investment income. They include investment income.

---

[11] Treasury Regulation Section 1.448-1T(f)(2)(iv)

> *Example 8.* If an employer generated $1,000,000 in each quarter in gross quarterly receipts but experienced $50,000 of sales returns, a $50,000 capital gain and $25,000 of interest income, the firm's gross receipts equal $1,025,000 for that quarter.

Tax-exempt Organization Gross Receipts

Tax-exempt organizations, however, use the meaning of gross receipts in Section 6033 rather than Section 448(c).

Under the Section 6033 regulations, "gross receipts" means the gross amount received by the organization from all sources without reduction for any costs or expenses including, for example, cost of goods or assets sold, cost of operations, or expenses of earning, raising, or collecting such amounts.

Thus, gross receipts includes, but is not limited to, the gross amount received as contributions, gifts, grants, and similar amounts without reduction for the expenses of raising and collecting such amounts, the gross amount received as dues or assessments from members or affiliated organizations without reduction for expenses attributable to the receipt of such amounts, gross sales or receipts from business activities (including business activities unrelated to the purpose for which the organization qualifies for exemption), the gross amount received from the sale of assets without reduction for cost or other basis and expenses of sale, and the gross amount received as investment income, such as interest, dividends, rents, and royalties.

PPP Forgiveness as Gross Receipts

If an employer received forgiveness on a Paycheck Protection Program (PPP) loan, that forgiveness counts as gross receipts. Technically. Fortunately, employers may exclude PPP loan forgiveness from their gross receipts.[12] The one requirement: An employer must show consistency in this accounting method.

Predictably, the "you can count or not count but be consistent" rule applies to shuttered venue operator grants and restaurant revitalization grants too.[13]

Note: Chapter 6 discusses the interplay of ERC and PPP loans in more detail.

When Employer Can't Compare to 2019

If the employer was not in existence as of the beginning of the same calendar quarter in calendar year 2019, it can look at 2020 instead of 2019.[14]

For example, an employer not in existence as of the beginning of the first calendar quarter of 2019, compares its first calendar quarter of 2021 gross receipts to its gross receipts in the first calendar quarter of 2020.

---

[12] Rev. Proc. 2021-33

[13] Revenue Procedure 2021-33

[14] IRS Notice 2021-23, page 6.

Similarly, an employer not in existence as of the beginning of the second calendar quarter of 2019, compares its second calendar quarter of 2021 gross receipts to its gross receipts in the second calendar quarter of 2020.

Alternative Quarter Comparison

An employer may also elect to use an alternative quarter method for gross receipts comparisons.

The alternative quarter method compares an employer's gross receipts for the immediately preceding calendar quarter with those for the corresponding calendar quarter in 2019 (substituting 2020 for 2019 if the employer did not exist as of the beginning of that quarter in 2019).

For example, to determine ERC eligibility for the first calendar quarter of 2021, an employer may elect to compare its gross receipts for the fourth calendar quarter of 2020 to the fourth calendar quarter of 2019.[15] In other words, eligibility for the first quarter of 2021 will not be based on that quarter's gross receipts but on the previous quarter's gross receipts.

> *Example 9.* An employer generated $1,000,000 of quarterly gross receipts through all four quarters of 2019, $700,000 of gross receipts in the fourth quarter of 2020, but then $2,000,000 of gross receipts in the first quarter of 2021. Notice that the first quarter's gross receipts of 2021, then, double the 2019 figures. This employer qualifies for ERC for the first quarter of 2021 using the alternative quarter method comparison.

---

[15] IRS Notice 2021-23, page 7.

If an employer was not in existence as of the beginning of the fourth calendar quarter of 2019, then the alternative quarter election will not be available for the first calendar quarter of 2021.

For the second calendar quarter of 2021, an employer may elect to use its gross receipts for the first calendar quarter of 2021 compared to those for the first calendar quarter of 2019 to determine if the decline in gross receipts test is met.

If an employer was not in existence as of the beginning of the first calendar quarter of 2019, then it may elect to measure the decline in gross receipts for the second calendar quarter of 2021 using its gross receipts for the first calendar quarter of 2021 compared to those for the first calendar quarter of 2020.

One final, interesting wrinkle related to the alternative quarter comparison. The election to use an alternative quarter isn't permanent. An employer could elect to use the alternative quarter comparison for the first quarter of 2021, but then return to using the usual quarter comparison the next quarter. The IRS provides this clarification in IRS Notice 2021-49, saying this:

> *The Treasury Department and the IRS have been asked whether an eligible employer must consistently use the alternative quarter election once it has made the election. As noted in section III.C. of Notice 2021-23, the determination of whether an employer is an eligible employer based on a decline in gross receipts is made separately for each calendar quarter. Thus, employers are not required to use the alternative quarter election consistently.*

Full Suspension Eligibility

If a federal, state or local government order fully suspends operations, "limiting commerce, travel, or group meetings (for commercial, social, religious, or other purposes) due to COVID-19,"[16] that order also qualifies an employer for employee retention credits.

The employer's eligibility runs for the interval of the suspension.

> *Example 10.* A government order causes a restaurant, a small eligible employer, to close from May 15 through August 15. The wages paid for that interval plug into the ERC formula. The employer does not, in other words, need to compare quarterly gross receipts.

IRS Notice 2021-20 describes exactly what counts as a government order, saying this on page 24:

> *Orders, proclamations, or decrees from the Federal government or any State or local government may be taken into account by an employer as "orders from an appropriate governmental authority" only if they limit "commerce, travel, or group meetings (for commercial, social, religious, or other purposes) due to the coronavirus disease 2019 (COVID-19)" and relate to the suspension of an employer's operation of its trade or business.*
>
> *Orders that are not from the Federal government must be from a State or local government that has jurisdiction over the employer's operations. These*

---

[16] See Section 2301(c)(2)(A)(ii)(I), as reproduced in Appendix for example.

> orders are referred to as "governmental orders." Whether orders, proclamations or decrees are governmental orders is determined without regard to the level of enforcement of the governmental order.

The notice also identifies what pronouncements and proclamations *fail to count* as an order, saying this:

> Statements from a governmental official, including comments made during press conferences or in interviews with the media, do not rise to the level of a governmental order for purposes of the employee retention credit. Additionally, the declaration of a state of emergency by a governmental authority is not sufficient to rise to the level of a governmental order if it does not limit commerce, travel, or group meetings in any manner. Further, such a declaration that limits commerce, travel, or group meetings, but does so in a manner that does not relate to the suspension of an employer's operation of its trade or business does not rise to the level of a governmental order for purposes of the employer's determination of its eligibility for the employee retention credit.

The notice specifically lists several things that do count:
- An order from the city's mayor stating that all non-essential businesses must close for a specified period;
- A State's emergency proclamation that residents must shelter in place for a specified period, other than residents who are employed by an essential business and who may travel to and work at the workplace location;

- An order from a local official imposing a curfew on residents that impacts the operating hours of a trade or business for a specified period;
- An order from a local health department mandating a workplace closure for cleaning and disinfecting.

A key issue that appears in the preceding list? Whether an employer's activities are deemed "essential." Helpfully, IRS Notice 2021-20 notes that whether the operations of a trade or business are considered essential or nonessential will often vary from jurisdiction to jurisdiction. And "an employer should determine whether it is operating an essential or non-essential business by referring to the governmental order affecting the employer's operation of its trade or business."[17]

And then two related issues to mention: the issue of consumer demand and the issue of comparable operations.

First, a reduction in consumer demand doesn't matter for purposes of determining full or partial suspension.[18] An employer suspending its operations in response to a decline in consumer demand doesn't result in ERC eligibility. Note however that if an employer sees a decline in consumer demand, it may qualify for ERC eligibility based on the substantial decline in gross receipts eligibility rule discussed earlier in the chapter.

---

[17] An employer claiming ERC eligibility on the basis of suspended operations needs to be able to substantiate the government order by producing a copy.

[18] This information appears in the Notice's "Question 13 and Answer 13" discussion.

A second complication to mention: IRS Notice 2021-20 says if an employer can run comparable operations despite a government order, that doesn't count. The notice gives a couple of good examples to highlight the nuances here. [19]

One example describes a software development firm. It reconfigures its operations to run comparably even after a local government order closes its offices. That firm, the IRS concludes, fails to qualify as fully or partially suspended.

Another example in that same discussion describes a physical therapy facility. This firm also reconfigures operations. But even reconfigured, it can't provide the full range of therapies. The closed facility provides equipment and tools that the physical therapists often need in hand to treat patients. That firm, the IRS concludes, qualifies as partially suspended.

Partial Suspension Eligibility

The earlier paragraphs have already introduced the idea of a partial suspension, so let's continue that discussion.

A partial suspension also triggers eligibility if the suspended operations represent more than a nominal portion of the employer's business. As with full suspension eligibility, the employer's ERC eligibility runs for the interval of the suspension.

---

[19] IRS Notice 21-20, Question 14 and Answer 14.

Further, a partial suspension may occur, thus triggering ERC eligibility, if an employer operates in multiple jurisdictions and some states or governments issue closure orders. Though this eligibility appears a little murkier to the author.

But let's start by talking about the "more than nominal" standard. And then we can get into the even muddier waters of an employer operating in multiple jurisdictions and under their various government orders.

More than Nominal Standard

According to the Treasury Department and IRS, a "more than nominal" portion of an employer's business operations would have generated ten percent or more of the firm's gross receipts in the same quarter of 2019. Or it would have amounted to ten percent or more of the firm's hours of service in the same quarter of 2019.[20]

Perhaps obviously, the partial suspension eligibility route exists because some employers don't need to fully suspend operations. An employer may for example operate both an essential business which may continue to operate. And it may operate a non-essential business which a government order suspends. In this case, the employer's partial suspension may create eligibility for employee retention credits.

---

[20] This information appears in the Notice's Question 12 and Answer 12" discussion.

> *Example 11.* A restaurant employer operates a dining room and cocktail lounge. If a government order closes the cocktail lounge due to COVID-19, that partial suspension qualifies the employer for employee retention credits if the cocktail lounge's gross receipts equal or exceed ten percent of the firm's total gross receipts. Or if the hours of service provided by the cocktail lounge staff equal or exceed ten percent of the firm's total hours worked. Note that the comparison looks back at the same quarter of 2019.

And here's another example, which may have been more common in many locations.

> *Example 12.* A restaurant provides both dine-in and take-out meals. If the COVID-19 pandemic causes a state or local government to close the restaurant's dining room, and dine-in gross receipts or hours of service from the same quarter of 2019 equaled or exceeded ten percent of the total gross receipts or total hours of service, that situation counts as a partial suspension.

Multiple Jurisdictions

If an employer operates in multiple locations and government orders close one of those locations, that closure appears to count, plain and simple, as a partial suspension.[21] Possibly even if the closed location is nominal. But it's murky.

In IRS Notice 2021-20, the following question is asked:

> *Is an employer that operates a trade or business in multiple locations and is subject to governmental orders requiring full or partial suspension of its*

---

[21] This information appears in the Notice's "Question 20 and Answer 20" discussion.

> operations in some jurisdictions, but not in others, considered to have a partial suspension of operations?

The notice then answers this question with an emphatic "Yes." But then the notice provides the following lengthy explanation which may not provide the clarity employers and their advisors seek:

> Employers that operate a trade or business in multiple locations and are subject to State and local governmental orders requiring full or partial suspension of operations in some, but not all, jurisdictions are considered to have a partial suspension of operations. Employers that operate a trade or business on a national or regional basis may be subject to governmental orders requiring closure of their locations in certain jurisdictions, but may not be subject to a governmental order in other jurisdictions. To operate in a consistent manner in all jurisdictions, these employers may establish a policy that complies with the local governmental orders, as well as the Center for Disease Control and Prevention (CDC) recommendations and the Department of Homeland Security (DHS) guidance; in this case, even though the employer may not be subject to a governmental order to suspend operations of its trade or business in certain jurisdictions, and may merely be following CDC or DHS guidelines in those jurisdictions, the employer would still be considered to have partially suspended operations due to the governmental orders requiring closure of its business operations in certain jurisdictions. Therefore, the employer would be an eligible employer with respect to all of its operations in all

> *locations for calendar quarters during which the employer's operations are partially suspended whether or not the employer voluntarily adopts consistent measures for its business operations in other jurisdictions.*

The preceding answer appears to say that if some jurisdictions in which an employer operates issue orders and the employer expands the closures based on CDC or DHS guidelines, that expansion of the original government orders works, too.

Unfortunately, the notice then immediately provides an example where it returns to looking at the "more than nominal" standard just mentioned (boldfacing added):

> *Employer L is a national retail store chain with operations in every state in the United States. In some jurisdictions, Employer L is subject to a governmental order to close its stores to customers, but is permitted to provide customers with curbside service to pick up items ordered online or by phone. In these jurisdictions, Employer L determines that it is not continuing comparable operations and that the stores that are closed to customers are **more than a nominal** portion of its business operations. In other jurisdictions, Employer L is not subject to any governmental order to close its stores to customers or is considered an essential business permitting its stores to fully remain open. Employer L establishes a company-wide policy, in compliance with the local governmental orders and consistent with the CDC and DHS recommendations and guidance, requiring the closure of all stores and operating with curbside pick-up only, even in those jurisdictions where the business was not subject to*

> *a governmental order. As a result of the governmental orders requiring closure of Employer L's stores to customers in certain jurisdictions, Employer L has a partial suspension of operations of its trade or business whether or not Employer L chooses to take consistent measures for stores in other jurisdictions. The partial suspension results in Employer L being an eligible employer nationwide for calendar quarters during which the employer's operations are partially suspended.*

Perhaps the safest takeaway here? It appears that an employer can expand government orders to achieve the "more than nominal" threshold if the rationale for the expansion reflects CDC and DHS recommendations and guidance.

Again, though, this area seems murky.

Recovery Start-up Business

For the third and fourth quarters of 2021, Section 3134 (see Appendix C) of tax law provides an unusual incentive to small business entrepreneurs: the recovery startup business employee retention credit.

How Recovery Start-up Business ERC Works

In a nutshell, the recovery startup business eligibility method gives an employer ERCs for starting a new trade or business. Chapter 4 talks about the issue of what counts as a new trade or business in detail. But the actual statute sets forth some pretty simple rules.

An employer gets ERCs if it starts a new trade or business after February 15, 2020 and if the employer's average annual gross receipts looking back at the three previous tax years before the quarter, do not exceed $1,000,000.

A taxpayer using calendar tax years, for example, needs its average annual gross receipts for 2018, 2019 and 2020 to not exceed $1,000,000.

An employer does not qualify for the recovery startup business category if it qualifies for employee retention credits due to substantial decline in gross receipts or full or partial suspension.

Finally, the employee retention credit laws treat tax-exempt organizations as trades or businesses. Accordingly, a tax-exempt employer who starts a new tax-exempt organization may be treated as starting a trade or business.

With that said, some examples help flesh out the details of this unusual incentive.

> *Example 13.* You open a restaurant on February 16, 2020. In this case you qualify. Note that had you opened one day earlier? You would not qualify. The recovery startup business ERC applies only in situations where you start a trade or business after February 15, 2020.

> *Example 14.* You operate an accounting firm and prepare people's taxes. So that's one trade or business. But on August 15, 2021, you open a second business, an equestrian center. Which represents another trade or business. You do qualify for the credit potentially because you began carrying on a trade or business (the new equestrian center) after February 15, 2020.

Regarding the three-year lookback to calculate average gross receipts: If an employer has less than three years of operation, it looks only at the years it operated.

> *Example 15.* If an employer didn't operate in 2018 or 2019 and so generated zero revenue for those years but started on January 1, 2020 and it generated $300,000 of revenue for that year, the average annual revenue equals $300,000. The reason? Because ($300,000/1) year equals $300,000.

If an employer operated for a short year, it annualizes that year's revenues.[22]

> *Example 16.* If an employer started on October 1, 2020 and it generated $300,000 of revenue for that last quarter, the average annual revenue equals $1,200,000. Essentially, $300,000 for a quarter equates to $1,200,000 for a year. That breaches the $1 million threshold and disqualifies the firm from using the ERC as a recovery startup business in 2021.

One other quick point to mention here. As mentioned already in earlier chapters, you need to aggregate all the businesses an owner or ownership group controls into a single employer. Chapter 5 discusses aggregation in detail. But for now, just understand that this consolidation occurs.

Due to this aggregation, the fictional tax accountant described in Example 14 faces a more complicated situation. Following a rule specified in Section 3134(d) and as mentioned earlier, she needs to aggregate the gross receipts from the businesses she operates. But say the tax accounting firm generated $400,000 in 2018, $800,000 in 2019, and $1,200,000 in 2020.

---

[22] Section 448(c)(3)(B)

Further suppose the equestrian center generated zero revenue in 2018, 2019 and 2020 because it only starts in 2021. In this case, the average gross receipts for the three years equals $800,000.

The following formula calculates the three-year average gross receipts in this example:

($400,000+$800,000+$1,200,000+$0+$0+$0)/3 years

The formula returns the result $800,000, and because $800,000 "does not exceed $1,000,000," she qualifies.

The Recovery Start-up Business Credit Limit

One final point to mention about the recovery startup business ERC. The recovery business startup ERC formula limits the quarterly benefit to $50,000.

Further, because the credit only works for the third and fourth quarter of 2021 — so two quarters — an employer would not receive more than $100,000 of recovery startup business ERCs.

Chapter 3: Qualified Wages

Chapter 2 describes the four methods an employer has for achieving ERC eligibility. But an employer eligible for employee retention credits, gets those credits *only* for paying qualified wages and allocable health benefits.

This chapter therefore describes what qualified wages and allocable qualified health benefits are and how an employer calculates these amounts.

Wages in General

For purposes of ERC, the definition of the term "wages" essentially matches everyday usage: wages represent amounts employers pay employees for their work.[23]

Probably, if an employer uses an outside payroll service such as ADP, Paychex or Gusto to handle employee payroll, the wages calculated and reported by that vendor represent wages which may plug into the ERC formula. (This would mesh with observations from our CPA practice.)

---

[23] Section 2301(c)(5) of the CARES Act and 3134(c)(4)(A) of the ARP define the term "wages" by referencing two chunks of tax law: Section 3121(a) and Section 3231(e). Section 3121(a) says and expounds on the theme that "the term 'wages' means all remuneration for employment." Section 3231(e) says that the "term 'compensation' means any form of money remuneration paid to an individual for services rendered as an employee to one or more employers."

An important point for employers of employees who receive tips—like restauranteurs: Wages include "cash tips received by an employee in any calendar month in the course of employment by an employer unless the amount of such cash tips is less than $20."[24]

Qualified Wages in 2020

Which "wages" count as "qualified wages," however, depends on the size of the employer organization. Furthermore, not everything you might guess counts actually "counts."

Employers with more than 100 Employees

If the average number of full-time employees employed by a firm during 2019 exceeds 100—what the Treasury Department and the IRS call a "large eligible employer"—qualified wages refer to amounts paid to employees not providing services due to COVID-19.

Note: Section 2301 uses the Section 4980H "Obamacare" definition of "full-time employee," so someone "employed on average at least 30 hours of service per week."

---

[24] IRS Notice 2021-49

> *Example 17.* Suppose you operate a trucking company that historically delivers food both to grocery stores and restaurants. The trucking company employed on average more than 100 full-time workers in 2019 and thus counts as a large eligible employer in 2020. Assume that half of your drivers deliver food to grocery stores (essential businesses that continue to receive food deliveries) and half the drivers deliver to restaurants (deemed nonessential businesses and which suspend food deliveries due to the COVID-19 crisis.) If you continue to a pay wages to truck drivers who used to deliver food to restaurants but who are now furloughed, those wages count as qualified wages for purposes of the employee retention credit formula.

Another example to consider: How the employee retention works for firms that simply laid-off employees the employer didn't need due to declining gross receipts.

> *Example 18.* Assume the same facts as in the preceding example but with one twist: You furlough or layoff all of the truck drivers who previously delivered food to restaurants. In this case, your firm pays no qualified wages. The wages paid to the truck drivers delivering food to grocery stores don't count. You don't get an employee retention credit.

One related wrinkle to know that applies to large eligible employers. Essentially, qualified wages may not exceed the amount an employee was paid for work during the 30 days immediately preceding eligibility.[25]

More specifically, the Treasury and IRS say this:

> *For large eligible employers, qualified wages paid to an employee may not exceed what the employee would have been paid for working an equivalent*

---

[25] Section 2301(c)(3)(B) sets this requirement.

duration during the 30 days immediately preceding the commencement of the full or partial suspension of the operation of the trade or business or the first day of the calendar quarter in which the employer experienced a significant decline in gross receipts. For a variable hour employee, the amount paid for working an equivalent duration during that 30-day period may be determined using any reasonable method. The method(s) that the Department of Labor has prescribed to determine the amount to pay an employee with an irregular schedule who is eligible for paid sick leave under the FFCRA would be considered reasonable for this purpose.

Example 19. Big Landscaping Company is a large eligible employer in 2020 because it on average employed more than 100 full-time employees in 2019. An employee earns $20 an hour of qualified wages while the firm is eligible for the employee retention credit. However, in the 30 days that precede the firm becoming eligible for ERC, the employee earned $15 an hour for the same work. In this situation, only $15 an hour of the employee's wages paid during the period of eligibility count as qualified wages.

Wage reductions don't count as qualified wages for ERC purposes. Wage reductions are simply "wage reductions."

> *Example 20.* A large professional services firm, responding to a government order that suspends non-essential operations, makes no reductions in its workforce. The firm does temporarily reduce all its employees' wages by ten percent. It reverses this wage cut once the government order ends. While the firm may be eligible for ERC due to a substantial decline in gross receipts or due to a government order suspending operations, it lacks qualified wages. No employee is paid for not providing services. Accordingly, it can claim no ERC.[26]

And one final thing to note: Employees that work less than 30 hours get ignored for purposes of determining whether an employer is a large eligible employer or a small eligible employer. Another way to say this same thing: No full-time equivalent calculation gets made. Note, however, wages paid to part-time employees may count for purposes of the ERC.[27]

> *Example 21.* A firm employs only ten full-time workers but one thousand part-time workers who work twenty hours each week. For purposes of determining whether the firm is a large or small eligible employer, the ERC rules look only at the ten full-time employees. The firm thus qualifies as a small eligible employer. Note, though, that potentially, all the wages it pays to full-time and part-time workers count toward ERC.

---

[26] See Question and Answer 36, Example 1 in IRS Notice 2021-20.

[27] IRS Notice 2021-49 makes this clarification, saying, "For purposes of determining whether an eligible employer is a large eligible employer or a small eligible employer, eligible employers are not required to include full-time equivalents when determining the average number of full-time employees. However, for purposes of identifying qualified wages, an employee's status as a full-time employee is irrelevant and wages paid to an employee who is not full-time may be treated as qualified wages if all other requirements to treat the amounts as qualified wages are satisfied."

Employers with 100 or Fewer Employees

The "qualified wages" definition works differently for employers with 100 or fewer employees.

First, for these employers, all wages paid while the firm maintains eligibility count as qualified wages.

> *Example 22.* Say you operate an ERC-eligible trucking company that delivers food both to grocery stores, (an essential business) and to restaurants (a nonessential business). Say that economic conditions require you to lay off all of your truck drivers who deliver food to restaurants, but say you continue to employ the shop employees and the truck drivers delivering food to grocery stores. Because you are a small eligible employer, you take the employee retention credit on all of the wages your firm pays. In other words, you get ERC on any wages you pay to the workers providing no services. And you get ERC on the wages you pay to workers providing services.

In addition, for a small eligible employer, no 30-day lookback period exists.

> *Example 23.* Little Landscaping Company is a small eligible employer because it on average employed less than 100 full-time employees in 2019. An employee earns $20 an hour of qualified wages while the firm is eligible for the employee retention credit. In the 30 days that precede the firm becoming eligible for ERC, the employee earned $15 an hour for the same work. But the firm still uses the $20 an hour of wages in the ERC formulas. The firm doesn't need to look back at the employee's 2019 wages.

Allocable Qualified Health Plan Expenses

ERC qualified wages include an eligible employer's allocable qualified health plan expenses.

More specifically, qualified wages include health plan expenses paid or incurred by an employer to provide and maintain a group health plan (as defined in Section 5000(b)(1) of the Internal Revenue Code), but only to the extent such amounts are excluded from the gross income of employees by reason of Section 106(a) of the tax code.

Allocable qualified health plan expenses do not include self-employed health insurance such as an S corporation shareholder employee might receive, employer contributions to health savings accounts (HSA), Archer Medical Saving Account (Archer MSA), or employer contributions to qualified small employer health reimbursement arrangement (QSEHRA).

Qualified health plan expenses do however include contributions to a health reimbursement arrangement (HRA) or a health flexible spending arrangement (health FSA).[28]

The Section 2301 statute doesn't specify how you're supposed to allocate what "allocable qualified health plan expenses" count as wages. But in IRS Notice 2021-20, the Treasury Department and the IRS give employers permission to use any reasonable method.[29]

An eligible employer who sponsors a fully-insured group health plan may use any reasonable method

---

[28] See IRS Notice 2021-20, in particular Question and Answer 46 and 47.

[29] See IRS Notice 2021-20, in particular Question and Answer 44

to determine and allocate the plan expenses, including (1) the COBRA applicable premium for the employee typically available from the insurer, (2) one average premium rate for all employees, or (3) a substantially similar method that takes into account the average premium rate determined separately for employees with self-only and other than self-only coverage.

Qualified Wages in 2021

The definition of a large eligible employer and small eligible employer changes for 2021.

Large Eligible Employer Definition Change

For 2021, a large eligible employer is a firm that employed on average more than 500 full-time workers in 2019.

This change obviously delivers an enormous new-for-calendar-year-2021 benefit to eligible employers with between 100 and 500 workers.

> *Example 24.* A firm employed on average 300 workers throughout 2019 and was ERC eligible due to partially suspended operations in the second, third and fourth quarter of 2020 and in the first and second quarter of 2021. Though the firm paid all 300 of its employees $10,000 each quarter in wages and qualified health plan expenses throughout this interval, it receives no ERC in 2020. The reason? Because it paid no employees to not work. In comparison, in 2021, the firm receives $2.1 million in credits in the first quarter and another $2.1 million in credits in the second quarter.

No 30-day Lookback for Large Eligible Employer

Another change for 2021: The 30-day lookback rule doesn't apply to large eligible employers in 2021.[30]

> *Example 25.* A large grocery store paid employees $15 an hour before they qualified for ERC due to a substantial decline in gross receipts. Throughout the pandemic, the store bumped employee wages by $5 an hour for hazard pay. For 2020, this large eligible employer only plugs $15 an hour into the ERC formulas, and thereby ignores the $5 an hour hazard pay. For 2021, however, the large eligible employer uses the full $20 an hour for its ERC calculations.

---

[30] IRS Notice 2021-23

Severely Financially Distressed Eligible Employer

And then one other change for large employers for the third and fourth quarter of 2021: The tweak to the qualified wages definition for severely financially distressed large eligible employers.[31] Quoting from IRS Notice 2021-49:

> *For purposes of the employee retention credit for the third and fourth calendar quarters of 2021, an eligible employer with gross receipts that are less than 10 percent of the gross receipts for the same calendar quarter in calendar year 2019 (or 2020, if the employer was not in existence in 2019) is a severely financially distressed employer.*

And what is key here, a severely financially distressed large-eligible employer, counts all its wages as qualified wages. So not just the wages paid to people for not working. But the wages paid to people for working.

> *Example 26.* Megacorp, a large eligible employer, sees its gross receipts for each of the quarters of the pandemic collapse to five percent of the gross receipts shown for the same quarters of 2019. Based on the substantial decline in gross receipts, Megacorp is an eligible employer with qualified wages in 2020 and 2021. For 2020 and the first two quarters of 2021, qualified wages include only the wages Megacorp paid to workers not providing services. For the third and fourth quarter of 2021, however, qualified wages include all the wages Megacorp paid to workers.

---

[31] Section 3134(c)(3)(C)

Qualified Wages Intervals

The period of eligibility determines the interval of time for which an employer has qualified wages.

For eligibility based on a substantial decline in gross receipts — an eligibility method that looks at quarterly gross receipts — an employer looks at and potentially counts all the wages and health insurance paid in each quarter of eligibility.

> *Example 27.* Due to a substantial decline in gross receipts, a commercial construction company qualifies for employee retention credits for the third and fourth quarter of 2020 and the first quarter of 2021. Potentially all of the wages and health plan expenses paid those quarters qualify and therefore plug into the ERC formula.

For eligibility based on full or partial suspension, an employer looks at and potentially counts wages and health insurance paid during the suspension.

> *Example 28.* A residential construction company qualifies for employee retention credits due to partial suspension of its operations during June and July of 2020. Potentially the wages and health plan expenses paid from June 1 through July 31 qualify and therefore plug into the ERC formula. So, the last month of the second quarter of 2020 and the first month of the third quarter of 2020.

For recovery startup business situations, the Treasury Department and IRS say that starting a trade or business within the quarter makes the employer eligible for all wages paid during the quarter.[32]

---

[32] Because this is nearly unbelievably beneficial for small business owners and entrepreneurs, we quote here the guidance from IRS Notice 2021-49, "Accordingly, in the third and fourth calendar quarters of 2021, a recovery startup business that is a small eligible employer within the meaning of section 3134(c)(3)(A)(ii) may treat

An example illustrates how this works:

> *Example 29.* The fictional commercial construction company from the preceding above doesn't qualify for employee retention credits based on a substantial decline in gross receipts after the first quarter of 2021. However, on the last day of the third quarter of 2021, the owner of the firm starts a new trade or business that meets the requirements of Section 3134(c)(5) for a recovery startup business. As a result, the owner becomes eligible for credits for both the third and fourth quarters of 2021.

The next chapter talks in more depth about how the recovery startup business works, and how business owners and entrepreneurs may want to exploit this tax planning opportunity.

Disqualified Wages

Not all wages qualify for ERC. Even for small eligible employers. The following paragraphs identify and briefly describe these situations.

Wages and Health Insurance Paid with PPP Funds

Wages paid using Paycheck Protection Program (PPP) funds don't qualify if the employer receives forgiveness.[33] Neither do wages paid with Shuttered Venue Operator Grants or Restaurant Revitalization Grants.[34]

---

all wages paid with respect to an employee during the quarter as qualified wages."

Chapter 6 discusses the interplay of the PPP and ERC programs in more detail. It also discusses how employers can apply for PPP forgiveness in a way that protects ERC refund claims. For now, however, readers can just remember that if an employer requests forgiveness for wages or health insurance paid with PPP funds, the employer implicitly elects to not claim ERC on those wages.

> *Example 30.* During the third and fourth quarters of 2020, an employer paid $200,000 in qualified wages that might have plugged into the ERC formulas. However, the employer received a $150,000 PPP loan and used $75,000 of that loan to pay wages and health insurance to employees during those quarters. The $75,000 of wages paid with PPP funds, essentially, get disqualified for use in the ERC formulas. As a result, the ERC qualified wages drop to $125,000.

Reduction in Qualified Wages from Other Credits

A handful of other credits exist and work similarly to the employee retention credit. With these other credits, the federal government fully or heavily subsidizes an employee's wages by providing tax credits an employer claims on its quarterly payroll tax returns.

---

[33] Originally, an employer could not both receive Paycheck Protection Program (PPP) funding and ERCs. The Consolidated Appropriations Act (2021) removed this requirement but it also created a predictable adjustment. An employer cannot claim ERC on wages or health insurance it paid using PPP money.

[34] Rev. Proc. 2021-33

In effect, these credits reduce qualified wages available for ERC. Mechanically, an employer ignores these other credits while determining qualified wages. But then the employer reduces the ERC for these credits.[35]

Owner and Owner Family Member Wages

In many cases, perhaps most cases, the wages paid to the business owner or to the family member of the business owner fail to count as qualified wages.[36] [37]

When Family Member Wages Get Disqualified

For example, the wages paid to following family members of a majority owner (like a sole proprietor or a shareholder who owns more than fifty percent of the shares of a corporation) don't count as qualified wages:

- A child or a descendant of a child
- A brother, sister, stepbrother, or stepsister
- The father or mother, or an ancestor of either

---

[35] Credits which reduce the ERC and therefore essentially reduce qualified wages include the credit described in Section 3111(e) of the Code, which permits qualified tax-exempt organizations that hire qualified veterans to claim a credit, Section 3111(f) of the Code, which permits a qualified small business to elect to apply part or all of its research credit available under Section 41 as an employment tax credit, and the credits described in Sections 7001 and 7003 of the Families First Coronavirus Response Act (FFCRA), which permit employers with fewer than 500 employees to claim as credits the wages paid to employees unable to work or telework due to certain circumstances related to COVID-19.

[36] IRS Notice 2021-49 explicitly provides this guidance, saying, "Section 2301(e) of the CARES Act and section 3134(e) of the Code provide, in relevant part, that rules similar to the rules of section 51(i)(1) of the Code apply. Section 51(i)(1) generally provides that wages paid to certain related individuals are not taken into account for purposes of the work opportunity credit."

[37] A sole proprietorship should not pay its owner wages. But if it did, those wages do not qualify for ERC.

- A stepfather or stepmother
- A niece or nephew
- An aunt or uncle
- A son-in-law, daughter-in-law, father-in-law, mother-in-law, brother-in-law, or sister-in-law
- An individual (other than a spouse, determined without regard to Section 7703, of the taxpayer) who, for the taxable year of the taxpayer, has the same principal place of abode as the taxpayer and is a member of the taxpayer's household

Constructive Ownership Determines Majority Owners

The ERC laws apply the constructive ownership logic of Section 267(c) to determine whether individual's ownership percentage rises to the level of a majority owner. This all gets a little gnarly, but in essence, three rules apply:[38]

Rule 1: An individual constructively owns their proportionate share of stock of a corporation owned, directly or indirectly, by or for a corporation, partnership, estate, or trust they own or have an interest in.

> *Example 31.* If John owns eighty percent of ABC corporation and ABC corporation owns eighty percent of DEF corporation, John constructively owns sixty-four percent of DEF corporation. Eighty percent of eighty percent equals sixty-four percent.

---

[38] Per Section 267(c) and as elaborated on in Notice 2021-49, "stock constructively owned by a person by reason of the application of Rule 1 will be treated, for the purpose of applying Rule 1, Rule 2, or Rule 3, as actually owned by that person. Stock constructively owned by an individual by reason of the application of Rule 2 or Rule 3 will not be treated as owned by the individual to again apply either rule to reattribute and make another individual the constructive owner of the stock."

Rule 2: An individual constructively owns the stock owned, directly or indirectly, by or for the individual's family. (An individual's family includes her or his brothers and sisters (both whole or half-blood), spouse, ancestors, and lineal descendants.)

> *Example 32.* If John is married to Mary and she owns one hundred percent of GHI corporation, John constructively owns one hundred percent of GHI corporation, too.

Rule 3: An individual who owns any stock in a corporation (other than through Rule 2's assumption) also constructively owns any stock owned, directly or indirectly, by or for his partner.

When Owner Wages Get Disqualified

Applying the rules mentioned in the preceding paragraphs, wages don't qualify for ERC if the majority owner has a living brother or sister (whether by whole or half-blood), living ancestor (parent or grandparent), or living lineal descendant (child or grandchild.)[39]

Bizarrely, owners in these situations find their wages disqualified because their ownership share is attributed to a family member and that attribution characterizes the owner as a family member of a majority owner.[40]

---

[39] See Section 267(c)(4) for full definitions.

[40] Here's the longer technical explanation from IRS Notice 2021-49: Applying the rules of sections 152(d)(2)(A)-(H) and 267(c) of the Code, a majority owner of a corporation is a related individual for purposes of the employee retention credit, whose wages are not qualified wages, if the majority owner has a brother or sister (whether by whole or half-blood), ancestor, or lineal descendant. That is, applying the constructive ownership rules of section 267(c), the direct majority owner's ownership of the corporation is attributed to each of the owner's family members with a relationship described in section 267(c)(4); further, because each of those family members is considered to own more than 50 percent of the stock of the corporation after applying section 267(c), the direct majority owner of the

When Owner's Spouse's Wages Get Disqualified

The owner's spouse's wages may often get disqualified, too. And for the same basic rule.

For example, if the business's majority owner has a living brother or sister (whether by whole or half-blood), a living ancestor, or a living lineal descendant (and thus is deemed to own the majority owner's shares under Section 267(c) of the Code) and the spouse bears a relationship included on the bulleted list on page 54 to the family member,[41] the spouse of the majority owner is a related individual for purposes of the employee retention credit. And in that case, the spouse's wages are not qualified wages.

In the event that the majority owner of a corporation has no living brother or sister (whether by whole or half-blood), no living ancestor, or no living lineal descendant as defined in Section 267(c)(4) of the Code, then neither the majority owner nor the spouse is a related individual within the meaning of Section 51(i)(1) of the Code. In this case, the wages paid to the majority owner and/or the spouse are qualified wages for purposes of the employee retention credit, assuming the other requirements for qualified wages are satisfied.

Note that the last few pages of IRS Notice 2021-49 provide a handful of examples showing how various constructive ownership arrangements affect qualified wages. A business owner wrestling with the constructive ownership riddle probably wants to carefully read that material.

---

corporation would have a relationship as defined in section 152(d)(2)(A)-(H) to the family member who is a constructive majority owner. Therefore, the direct majority owner is a related individual for purposes of the employee retention credit.

[41] The list comes from described in section 152(d)(2)(A)-(H) of the Internal Revenue Code.

Chapter 4: Start-up Trades or Businesses

As briefly noted in Chapter, 2, a third category of employers become eligible for the employee retention credit for the third and fourth calendar quarters of 2021: recovery startup businesses.[42]

Unfortunately, however, this method of ERC eligibility burdens business owners and their professional advisors with significant complexities and uncertainties. Business owners and advisors therefore want to carefully parse the definition of the trade or business, thoughtfully determine exactly when a new trade or business starts, understand the murkiness that exists when a business with one trade or business starts a second trade or business, and then also stay alert to the issue of an activity representing a hobby.

ERC Trade or Business Definition

The Treasury Department and IRS provide some useful guidance on what a "trade or business" is for purposes of ERC.

In IRS Notice 2021-49, for example, they say this:

> *for purposes of the employee retention credit, "trade or business" has the same meaning as when used in section 162 of the Code other than*

---

[42] Section 3134(c)(2)(A)(ii)(III)

> *the trade or business of performing services as an employee.*

And then also this:

> *In general, for purposes of section 162, a taxpayer has not begun carrying on a trade or business "until such time as the business has begun to function as a going concern and performed those activities for which it was organized."*

The guidance from the Treasury Department and IRS references two court cases and an old revenue ruling, which elaborate on the question of when a business owner or entrepreneur's activities and efforts move beyond pre-opening and planning and constitute an operational trade or business.

The first court case, for example, talks about entrepreneurs starting a Richmond Virginia television station in the 1950s.[43] In this case, the court decides the taxpayer's business doesn't incur ordinary and necessary expenses until they actually receive the needed broadcasting license from the Federal Communications Commission (FCC) and begin television broadcasting.

The twin points the Treasury Department and IRS seem to be making here: First, a recovery startup business possibly goes through a pre-opening, or startup phase, during which time, the trade or business clearly has not yet started. Second, a recovery startup business needs to clearly be operating. In the case of a television station, for example, the business needs to have not only secured the necessary licenses from the FCC, it also needs to have begun broadcasting.

---

[43] Richmond Television Corp. v. U.S., 345 F.2d 901, 907 (4th Cir. 1965)

The second court case talks about a bank holding company that spends money exploring new metropolitan markets within the state where it operates.[44] The IRS argues in this case that the bank spending (on things like market studies and feasibility studies) to expand its banking trade or business to new retail locations fails to count as ordinary and necessary expenses. In this case, the court decides these expenditures to expand the existing trade or business clearly do count. The point the Treasury Department and IRS may be making here: The expansion of an existing trade or business doesn't create recovery startup business eligibility.

Revenue Ruling 81-150, the other source cited in the notice, discusses a partnership formed to drill offshore for oil. In that case, the IRS rules the partnership incurs no ordinary and necessary expenses until it begins drilling. The apparent message here echoes the message of the Richmond Television Corp case: A startup business needs to begin operating as a going concern in order to establish eligibility for ERCs.

The Section 162 Trade or Business Meaning

Section 162, it's useful to note, doesn't define what a trade or business is. Rather, Section 162 says taxpayers can deduct the ordinary and necessary expenses of running a trade or business–and then it and the related regulations describe the detailed rules for taking these deductions.

---

[44] NCNB Corporation v. United States, 684 F.2d 285 (4th Cir. 1982)

However, when the Treasury Department, the IRS and tax practitioners throw around the term "Section 162 trade or business," what they *really* mean is an activity that the courts and the Internal Revenue Service in past decisions count as a real trade or business that generates legitimate Section 162 business deductions.

An old seminal court decision still gives a nice overview of the issues, Groetzinger v. IRS Commissioner. Groetzinger was a professional gambler who wanted to deduct his losses as business expenses. In the word, the court agreed.

But what's useful about Groetzinger to readers of this book? Groetzinger describes what a Section 162 trade or business needs to look. The activity needs to be continuous and not sporadic. And the activity needs to be conducted with regularity and with a profit motive.

Interestingly, and usefully, the Schedule C instructions, which tell a sole proprietor how to report the income and deductions, echo this theme.[45] The *very* first two sentences of the instructions say this:

> *Use Schedule C (Form 1040) to report income or (loss) from a business you operated or a profession you practiced as a sole proprietor. An activity qualifies as a business if your primary purpose for engaging in the activity is for income or profit and you are involved in the activity with continuity and regularity.*

---

[45] The 2020 Schedule C Instructions appear here: https://www.irs.gov/pub/irs-pdf/i1040sc.pdf

When a Start-up Business Actually Starts

The precise point at which the business starts matters. In order to claim ERC for the third quarter and fourth quarter of 2021, an employer needs to start a new trade or business sometime after February 15, 2020[46] but no later than September 30, 2021.[47]

If an employer starts a new trade or business during the fourth quarter of 2021, it may not claim an ERC for the third quarter of 2021. But it may claim ERC for the fourth quarter if the new trade or business starts by December 31, 2021.

To amplify the logic of the two court cases and the revenue ruling cited above, preopening activities which occur prior to the point in time the business starts *fail* to qualify a firm for the ERC.

> *Example 33.* A new entrepreneur wants to open her first restaurant. She spends the summer and fall of 2021 developing a menu, building out a new restaurant and kitchen, and training kitchen and wait staff. Between June of 2021 and December of 2021, in fact, she spends hundreds of thousands of dollars on wages. Because the restaurant doesn't open until January 1, 2022, she fails to qualify as an eligible employer. Had she opened a day earlier—on New Year's Eve—she would have qualified for the fourth quarter for 2021.

---

[46] Section 3134(c)(5)(A)

[47] IRS Notice 2021-49

Starting a Second Trade or Business

To clear up a point of possible confusion, an employer definitely can start a new trade or business. Internal Revenue Code Sections explicitly discuss rules for situations where a taxpayer or employer owns multiple trades or businesses.[48] The Schedule C instructions quoted earlier also reflect this understanding.[49] In terms of the recovery startup business ERC, three additional factors push one to this conclusion:

Gross Receipts Allowed in Three Preceding Tax Years

For one thing, consider the requirement that an eligible employer qualifying for ERC needs to average gross receipts for the three prior years of not more than $1,000,000. That strongly suggests an eligible employer already operates a trade or business.

---

[48] See Section 446, for example, and the associated regulations.

[49] Page C-3 and C-10 of the Schedule C form instructions echo this, and talk about situations where a taxpayer must explicitly recognize it may operate multiple trades or businesses.

Qualified Wages May Be Incurred Prior to Starting

For another thing, consider the instruction in IRS Notice 2021-49 that says all the wages paid during the quarter count for ERC if the eligible employer starts a new trade or business during the quarter. That indicates an eligible employer may also be paying wages for other trades or businesses before the new startup business commences operations.

Statutory and Regulatory Language

A final thing to consider: If one reads the statutes, and the three IRS notices that talk about eligible employers, and one considers this question while reading, careful readers reasonably conclude an eligible employer with an existing trade or business (or several trades or businesses) may start a new trade or business.

Related to Section 3134 statute, for example, consider the Section 3134(c)(5)(A) phrase,

> *which begin carrying on any trade or business after February 15, 2020.*

Congress wouldn't need to use the phrase "any trade or business" if an employer can operate only a single trade or business.

If an employer can operate only a single trade or business, it seems like Congress should have used phrasing such as "its trade or business" or "the trade or business" or even just "operations," as shown below:

> which begin carrying on its trade or business after February 15, 2020.

The point to take away then? An employer may operate more than one trade or business. And in terms of the ERC, an employer with one or more *existing* trades or businesses may become an eligible employer by starting yet another *new* trade or business.

New Trade or Business Planning Tips

To claim the recovery startup business ERC, I think taxpayers with existing trades or businesses want to think about three issues that all get pretty tangled up in any real-life situation:
- *Starting* a new trade or business
- *Timing* the start so it leads to an ERC
- *Separating* the trade or business from other existing trades or businesses.

Show Something is Starting

In terms of fully starting a new trade or business, taxpayers may want to take steps that explicitly illustrate something new is starting. And several common-sense ideas spring to mind for clearly showing something is starting.

A good case, I think, can be made for having a formal business plan. That action not only creates documentation that shows the business owner is starting a new venture. It very possibly helps the business owner differentiate the new venture from the existing venture.

A new legal entity, such as a new limited liability company or new corporation, may help flag, or help establish, the *start* of the new trade or business.[50] [51]

> *Example 34.* Consider the example of a restaurateur who currently operates an Italian restaurant and wants to start a new French restaurant. If the business owner uses one corporation for the Italian restaurant and another corporation for the French restaurant, that ownership may strengthen the case that the French restaurant represents a new trade or business starting.

Finally, much useful guidance exists on what expenses represent preopening expenditures and when a firm obviously fits into a pre-startup phase. Entrepreneurs often attempt to avoid or minimize these qualities to accelerate the date they can begin deducting expenses.[52]

However, in terms of ERC, obvious preopening expenditures and a clear-cut startup phase may prove helpful. The start-up phase may make more apparent the start of the actual business.

> *Example 35.* A restaurateur operating an Italian restaurant wants to start a new French restaurant. If the new French restaurant incurs measurable expenses developing its menu and training wait and kitchen staff, that preopening and startup activity strengthens the argument that the new French restaurant starts the night it first serves patrons.

---

[50] Treasury Regulation 1.195, in particular its language that the taxpayer starting a trade or business (so the corporation that owns a business) makes the elections about how to handle startup expenditures. Also see the instructions for when to deduct startup expenditures in IRS Publication 535 on page 4.

[51] See Gold-Pak Meat Co., T.C. Memo. 1971-83 and then also Morton, 98 Fed. Cl. 596 (2011), which show both sides of this coin.

[52] Section 195 and the related Treasury Regulations.

Explicitly Document the Timing Works

As just noted, the usual rules for startup expenditures delay the point a business begins deducting expenses until the business has fully started. Often a delay of a few days doesn't matter much to either the taxpayer or the IRS. A tax deduction might just move into the next tax year.

With the ERC, however, a delay of a few days may matter a lot. A delay may mean an employer loses the ERC for the quarter.

Accordingly, anything an employer can do to create evidence of the trade or business starting in time to qualify probably helps: press releases, local news coverage, grand openings, big splashy sales for shoppers and so forth.

Further in this vein, the 81-150 revenue ruling mentioned by IRS Notice 2021-49 suggests an idea, I think. That revenue ruling talks about an offshore drilling platform. And while that ruling relates to the very specific case of a manufacturer running a production trade or business, it suggests that merely placing assets into service fail to count. The assets that comprise the essence of the new trade or business need to be fully used.

> *Example 36.* A caterer who decides to start a restaurant gets the restaurant open and all the necessary permits in place by December 31, 2021. She also begins to use the new restaurant location's kitchen over the Christmas holidays for catering (so her existing trade or business). On New Year's Eve, she rents the restaurant out for a private party. While the kitchen and the dining have been placed into service in this scenario, one should probably question whether the restaurant trade or business has started. I think not. And even if private parties represent a regular event.

One last comment about explicitly documenting that the timing of the start works for the ERC. I would think that business practices like so-called "soft launches" or "beta versions" of products or services damage the argument a new trade or business has actually already started and so validly takes the ERC.

An employer wants to avoid any appearance the trade or business was only sort of, partially, kind of half open…

Clearly Separating New Trade or Business

In terms of separating a new identifiable trade or business from an existing trade or business, several factors can be used for differentiation.

Different activities—reflected in different North American Industry Classification System (NAICS) codes, being reported on the tax return when possible—suggest a different activity and therefore possibly a new trade or business.[53]

---

[53] See Tax Advisor April 1, 2019 article, "Exploring the undefined: Trade or Business, " By Erica L. Parra, J.D., LL.M., and Darian A. Harnish, CPA, and then

Different trades or businesses would logically employ different workers and use different assets. That would be a factor to consider.

Different trades or businesses might often operate in different geographic locations. And probably the more geographic separation, the better?[54] That would lend an aura of separateness.

Actions taken to expand an existing trade or business fail to count as a new trade or business, according the NCNB Corporation court decision cited in IRS Notice 2021-49. Accordingly, and purely for purposes of ERC, an eligible employer might want to avoid new trades or businesses where obvious synergies exist.

> *Example 37.* An entrepreneur who owns and operates a restaurant is considering starting another business. But she has two attractive options. A catering business, and a clothing boutique. Possibly the catering business—which might use staff and facilities from and sell to the same customers as the restaurant—fails to count as new trade or business. In comparison, the new clothing boutique probably does count as a new trade or business.

Tax law requires a taxpayer to keep a separate or separable set of books and financial records for each trade or business. Accordingly, a taxpayer who does that—who keeps separate or separable books and records—should more effectively differentiate a new trade or business from existing trades or businesses.[55]

---

one of the cases it references, Marlin Grocery Co.,15 B.T.A. 1080 (1929)

[54] See Nielsen, 61 T.C. 311 (1973), for example, where two hospitals operating in different locations are deemed separate trades or businesses even though they share some employees.

The Richmond Television Corp court decision referenced by IRS Notice 2021-49 talks some about the FCC license the business owner needs in order to begin television broadcasting. That requirement to have to first procure a license would seem to suggest a new trade or business. And it would also create a starting line to show when a trade or business begins.

The aggregation rules consolidate the trades or businesses an eligible employer's ownership group operates. (The next chapter talks about these rules.) But a different ownership group *starting up* might tend to reflect a new activity and therefore a new trade or business *starting up*.

> *Example 38.* A father and son work together in a residential home construction business owned by the father. If the father and son form a new partnership that constructs fences, that would seem to represent a new trade or business.

Avoiding Hobby Taint

One final, negative factor to consider: The possible taint of something that arguably resembles a hobby. Or an activity that fails to show a clear profit motive on the part of the owner.

---

[55] Treasury Regs. Sec. 1.446-1(d)(2), says this, "No trade or business will be considered separate and distinct for purposes of this paragraph unless a complete and separable set of books and records is kept for such trade or business."

The Section 162 definition of a trade or business requires a profit motive. A hobby fails that requirement. And obviously, an activity started merely to qualify for ERCs also fails that requirement.

One wonders if some small business entrepreneurs will find their new trade or business fails to produce ERCs because the venture simply doesn't rise to the level of a trade or business: An activity with a profit motive, and then regular and continuous involvement.

The following example illustrates this situation:

> *Example 39.* A taxpayer operates a small law firm that barely qualifies as an eligible employer if the taxpayer starts a recovery startup business. Nevertheless, the taxpayer starts two new businesses. He uses his sailboat to give rides to tourists. He also begins driving for Uber, which he grudgingly does only a handful of weekends. Arguably, the sailboat ride business fails to count as a trade or business because that activity is a hobby. Arguably, starting a small ride-sharing business fails to count—probably both because the business owner isn't motivated by profit and then fails to show continuity and regularity.

Chapter 5: How Aggregation Works

The ERC statutes require employers to aggregate the businesses which the same ownership group controls.

If an entrepreneur owns one hundred percent of three corporations, the ERC formulas combine those three corporations, treating them as a single employer.

And this important point: Aggregation can both help and hurt, in terms of maximizing employee retention credits.

This chapter explains how aggregation works and points readers to the technical resources that give the precise rules. I will say this, however: If you face a situation where you need to aggregate, you probably want to make sure the aggregation gets performed by someone skilled.

Further, if you're the "someone skilled" doing the work you're probably going to need to trace your way through the Treasury Regulation examples (which I'll discuss briefly in the pages that follows.)

Where Aggregation Matters

To start, let's quickly review where aggregation matters. For starters, aggregation matters in terms of the per employee credit.

> *Example 40.* John works for two corporations that get aggregated because they both have the same owner. John earned $10,000 in wages working at each corporation. Without aggregation, each corporation might get a $5,000 credit, or fifty percent of the $10,000 of wages each paid in 2020. For ERC purposes, however, only the first $10,000 of wages qualify for the credit. That $5,000 credit therefore gets shared between the two corporations. Probably each will get a $2,500 credit for wages they paid John.

Aggregation affects the count of full-time employees and so may influence whether a firm is a large employer or a small employer.

> *Example 41.* An entrepreneur constructively owns one hundred percent of two businesses. One operates as a corporation. One operates as partnership. To make the ERC calculations, the entrepreneur aggregates the two businesses and treats them as a single employer. If the corporation employed 100 full-time workers in 2019 and the partnership employed 100 full-time workers in 2019, the aggregated entity is treated as having employed 200 full-time workers in 2019. That means that for 2020, the ERC laws categorize the employer as a large eligible employer and that for 2021, the ERC laws categorize the employer as small eligible employer.

Note: As discussed in Chapter 3, for 2020 large eligible employers employ more than 100 full-time workers. And for 2021, large eligible employers employ more than 500 full-time workers.

The aggregation also applies when determining whether an employer gains eligibility for ERC based on a substantial decline in gross receipts.

> *Example 42.* Two sisters together own two restaurants with the older sister owning eighty percent and the younger sister owning twenty percent. In 2019, each restaurant generated $1,000,000 of gross receipts. In 2020, due to COVID-19, one restaurant sees its gross receipts drop to $300,000 while the other restaurant sees its gross receipts drop to $900,000. On an aggregated basis, therefore, the combined restaurants' gross receipts drop from $2,000,000 in 2019 to $1,200,000 in 2020. But that forty percent decline fails to qualify the aggregated firm for ERC based on a substantial decline in gross receipts. (For 2020, an employer needs to suffer a decline of more than fifty percent.)

Finally, the aggregation applies when assessing whether an employer experiences either full or partial suspension due to government orders.

> *Example 43.* Returning to the preceding example where two sisters own a couple of restaurants, if the 2020 revenues drop due to government orders which close their dine-in business and those orders last from April 1 through December 31, the aggregated firm almost certainly qualifies as partially suspended from April through December. A partial suspension requires a government order that closes a more nominal component of the business. More than nominal means ten percent or more. Almost surely, the one restaurant suffering the drop in gross receipts from $1,000,000 to $300,000 because it closed its dining room, allows the aggregated employer to use the partial suspension rules.

When Employers Get Aggregated

The ERC statutes use two Internal Revenue Code Sections to aggregate firms: Section 52, which is for controlled group of corporations, and Section 414(m), which is for affiliated service groups.

And a caution: These statutes require careful reading and precise application.

Section 52 Controlled Group of Corporation

Section 52 says essentially two things. First, that all the employers part of a controlled group of corporations count as a single employer. Second, that employers of partnerships and sole proprietorships are treated like employees of corporations for this determination.[56] (In essence, Section 52 treats partnerships and sole proprietors as corporations for grouping purposes.)

Three arrangements count as controlled group of corporations:[57]
- A *parent-subsidiary controlled group of corporations,* which is one or more chains of corporations where the common parent corporation owns more than 50 percent of the total combined voting power of all classes of stock entitled to vote, or more than 50 percent of the value of all classes of stock of each corporation.[58]

---

[56] Section 52(a) and Section 52(b) reference Section 1563(a) and tweak Section 1563(a)'s controlling percentage from eighty percent to more than fifty percent.

[57] IRS Notice 2021-20

- A *brother-sister controlled group of corporations,* which is two or more corporations where (1) five or fewer persons who are individuals, estates, or trusts own at least 80 percent of the total combined voting power of all classes of stock entitled to vote, or the total value of shares of all classes of stock of each corporation; and (2) the same five or fewer persons, taking into account ownership only to the extent that it is identical with respect to each corporation, own more than 50 percent of the total voting power of all classes of stock entitled to vote, or total value of shares of all classes of stock of each corporation.[59]
- A *combined group of corporations,* which is three or more corporations, each of which is a member of either a parent-subsidiary or a brother-sister controlled group, and at least one of which is both the common parent of a parent-subsidiary controlled group and also a member of a brother-sister controlled group.[60]

This tip: The Treasury Regulations for Section 1563, so the Section which Section 52 references, provides numerous examples of when a controlled group of corporations exist.

Someone tasked with the job of deciding what corporations should be aggregated probably needs to work from these examples.[61]

[58] Treasury Regulation 1.52-1.

[59] Ibid

[60] Ibid

[61] Treasury Regulation 1.1563-1. It provides seventeen examples.

Section 414(m) Affiliated Service Group

Section 414(m) treats the employees working for members of an affiliated service as employed by a single employer. Section 414(m) describes three types of affiliated service groups. The first and second types of affiliated service groups are described under section 414(m)(2) and require a combination of common ownership and performance of services among certain organizations. The third type is described under section 414(m)(5), requires no common ownership, and aggregates employers based on the performance of management functions by one organization for another organization (and related organizations).

If you either own or advise entities that comprise an affiliated service group, you'll need to review the statutes and aggregate as appropriate.

Tribes and Tribal Entities

Aggregation logically applies to tribes, tribal governments and other tribal entities because these entities enjoy full eligibility for ERC.[62] Unfortunately, however, the IRS says little--only that tribe and tribal entity employers should use a "reasonable, good faith interpretation in determining how the aggregation rules apply."[63]

---

[62] IRS Notice 2021-20, Question and Answer 3.

[63] IRS Notice 2021-20, Quicken and Answer 9

When Employer Acquires a Trade or Business

One last aggregation topic needs to be briefly discussed: What happens when an employer acquires a trade or business during 2020 or 2021.

IRS Notice 2021-20 provides the rule here. It says that if an employer that acquires (in an asset purchase, stock purchase, or any other form of acquisition) a trade or business during 2020, the acquirer includes the gross receipts from the acquired business in its gross receipts computation for each calendar quarter that it owns and operates the acquired business.

However, the Treasury Department and IRS offer employers an interesting accounting option—which may work to the employer's benefit. For purposes of making comparisons to 2019's quarterly revenues—such as for determining whether or not a substantial decline in gross receipts has occurred—the new aggregated employer can consider gross receipts before ownership begins.

It makes sense to quote here the notice's language because this aggregation technique potentially provides a significant planning opportunity for some employers:

> *Solely for purposes of the employee retention credit, when an employer compares its gross receipts for a 2020 calendar quarter when it owns an acquired business to its gross receipts for the same calendar quarter in 2019, the employer may, to the extent the information is available, include the gross receipts of the acquired business in its gross receipts for the 2019 calendar quarter. Under this safe harbor approach, the employer*

> *may include these gross receipts regardless of the fact that the employer did not own the acquired business during that 2019 calendar quarter.*

If an employer acquires a trade or business in the middle of a quarter, and it chooses to use the method described in the preceding quotation, it must "estimate the gross receipts it would have had from that acquired business for the entire quarter based on the gross receipts for the portion of the quarter that it owned and operated the acquired business."

An employer may choose not to use the above method, which the notice terms a "safe harbor." In that case, the employer looks only at gross receipts after it owns and operates the acquired trade or business.

But Notice 2021-20 provides example showing how this aggregation works, which appears below. And you definitely want to know how this accounting trick works if it applies to your situation because it may allow you to qualify for ERC:

> *Employer D acquired all of the assets of a trade or business in a taxable transaction on January 1, 2020. The gross receipts of the acquired business were $50,000 for the quarter beginning January 1, 2020, and ending March 31, 2020, and $200,000 for the quarter beginning January 1, 2019, and ending March 31, 2019. Employer D has access to the books and records from the prior owner of the acquired trade or business and can determine the amount of gross receipts attributable to the trade or business for the quarter beginning January 1, 2019, and ending March 31, 2019. For purposes of the employee retention credit, Employer D must include $50,000 in its gross receipts computation for the quarter beginning January 1, 2020, and ending March 31, 2020 (because Employer D actually owned the trade or business) and may include $200,000 in its gross receipts computation for the quarter beginning January 1, 2019, and ending March 31, 2019*

Chapter 6: Balancing ERC and PPP

If an employer received a Paycheck Protection Program (PPP) loan, forgiveness of that PPP loan affects the ERC formulas.

The reason for this impact? A PPP borrower gets forgiveness for spending PPP funds on wages. But whatever wages the borrowers uses for that forgiveness? A borrower loses the ability to plug those specific wages into the ERC formula.

> *Example 44.* A small business potentially qualifies for $50,000 of employee retention credits in 2020 on $100,000 of wages and qualified health expenses due to partial suspension. If this small business received a $100,000 PPP loan, the borrower might get full forgiveness for using the funds for $100,000 of W-2 wages. And it might, just to be efficient, show that same $100,000 of W-2 wages on its PPP forgiveness application. But in that case, it qualifies for no employee retention tax credit on those wages. The business can't use the same wages for PPP forgiveness and employee tax credits.

For this reason, how a PPP borrower fills out her, his or their PPP loan forgiveness application really matters.

This chapter therefore explains in general terms how PPP loans and PPP loan forgiveness work.

And then it makes suggestions for filling out a PPP forgiveness application in a manner that leads to full forgiveness but that also salvages as much as possible any ERCs.

Review of the PPP Loan Formula

A brief review of the PPP loan formula makes sense.
The PPP loan formula looked at the annual payroll and related costs an employer paid, (including group health care benefits and retirement plan contributions), calculated the average monthly payroll amount, and then loaned 2.5 months of that average monthly payroll amount to the employer.[64]

> *Example 45.* An employer pays ten employees $60,000 a year and pays the owner $100,000 a year. The employer also provides group health insurance which costs $50,000 annually, and it provides employee retirement benefits of $30,000 a year. The total annual payroll costs equal $780,000 in this case. The average monthly payroll costs equal $65,000 in this case. Assuming a borrower qualified for a PPP loan, the loan amount probably equaled 2.5 times $65,000, or $162,500.

Review of the PPP Forgiveness Formula

The PPP forgiveness formula looks both at payroll costs and at nonpayroll costs.

---

[64] First draw PPP loans equaled 2.5 times the average monthly payroll costs. And probably many second draw PPP loans also equaled 2.5 times the average monthly payroll. Some second draw PPP loans were larger, however. If a PPP borrower operated a business classified under Code 72 of the North American Industry Classification System (for example, a hotel, restaurant or bar), the second draw PPP equaled 3.5 times the average monthly payroll costs.

But payroll costs appear at the center of the forgiveness formula. That formula requires a PPP borrower to spend at least sixty percent of the PPP loan on payroll costs during the covered period—which usually ran 24 weeks starting on the date the PPP loan funded.

General Rule Regarding PPP Payroll

The Small business Administration (SBA) and Treasury Department initially summarized the statutory definition of payroll costs for PPP loans this way:[65]

> *Payroll costs consist of compensation to employees (whose principal place of residence is the United States) in the form of salary, wages, commissions, or similar compensation; cash tips or the equivalent (based on employer records of past tips or, in the absence of such records, a reasonable, good-faith employer estimate of such tips); payment for vacation, parental, family, medical, or sick leave; allowance for separation or dismissal; payment for the provision of employee benefits consisting of group health care coverage, including insurance premiums, and retirement; payment of state and local taxes assessed on compensation of employees; and for an independent contractor or sole proprietor, wages, commissions, income, or net earnings from self-employment, or similar compensation.*

---

[65] The first paragraphs of Section 636(a)(36) supply the actual definition, but see footnote Federal Register / Vol. 85, No. 105 / Rules and Regulations, page 33005.

The Continuing Small Business Recovery and Paycheck Protection Program Act added to this list by saying that other group insurance benefits should be counted, too.[66]

Further, the follow-up rules, form instructions, and "Frequently Asked Questions" documents—discussed in the pages of this chapter—fill in many details. But a general principle appears—and then an exception.

That principle: Payroll and related costs appear on a business' income tax return. For example, the salary and wages reported on a Schedule C form used by a sole proprietor, a partnership 1065 return, an 1120 C corporation return, or an 1120S S corporation represent the "cash compensation" costs the PPP formulas focus on.

Similarly, the health insurance and other group insurance employee-fringe-benefit deductions reported on a Schedule C form or on a 1065, 1120, or 1120S tax return count as the group insurance that can be plugged into the PPP formulas.

The same rule applies to retirement benefits. If the business deducts the pension expense on its Schedule C, 1065, 1120, or 1120S tax return, the amount counts as a payroll cost for PPP purposes.

Finally, the state and local payroll taxes that count for PPP purposes get deducted along with other payroll taxes on these same business tax returns.

---

[66] Section 105, Continuing Small Business Recovery and Paycheck Protection Program Act.

Note that not every dollar reported in one of these tax deduction categories count for purposes of the Paycheck Protection Program. But if a payroll or related cost is "PPP-worthy," the cost shows up as a deduction in one of these locations.

Exception to the General Payroll Rule

An exception to the general rule just described occurs. Congress wrote the statutes to not just provide employees with "payroll protection" but also to provide business owners with replacement compensation. (See the last lines of the earlier quotation.) Sole proprietors and partners earn self-employment income, however. They do not receive wages from an employer.

Accordingly, for these situations, the SBA crafted a clever work around. The SBA says a sole proprietor generally looks at her or his Schedule C form from 2019. The exact instruction appears in several places, including the "How to Calculate Maximum Loan Amounts" document that the Treasury and SBA published at their websites. That document, quoted below, says a sole proprietors owner's compensation equals his or her:[67]

---

[67] This instruction appears on Page 2 of How to Calculate Maximum Loan Amounts – By Business Type document which is available at the U.S. Treasury website: **https://home.treasury.gov/system/files/136/How-to-Calculate-Loan-Amounts.pdf.**

> ...*2019 IRS Form 1040 Schedule C line 31 net profit amount (if you have not yet filed a 2019 return, fill it out and compute the value)...*

And then the SBA provides a similar rule for partners in active trades or businesses saying a partner's owner compensation equals her or his:

> ...*2019 Schedule K-1 (IRS Form 1065) Net earnings from self-employment of individual U.S. based general partners that are subject to self-employment tax, computed from box 14a (reduced by any section 179 expense deduction claimed, unreimbursed partnership expenses claimed, and depletion claimed on oil and gas properties) multiplied by 0.9235...*

Note, then, that the SBA provides formulas for sole proprietors and partnerships to develop a reasonable owner compensation replacement amount these borrowers can plug into both the PPP loan amount formula and the forgiveness calculations.

Employers looking to present PPP forgiveness information in a manner that salvages ERC qualified wages need to pay particularly close attention to the owner compensation amounts. Those amounts usually don't count (almost never count?) as qualified wages. But they produce lots of payroll costs for PPP borrowers.

The PPP Nonpayroll Costs

Valid, nonpayroll PPP costs include a bunch of different spending categories. An employer seeking to maximize its ERC refunds wants to understand how to maximize the nonpayroll costs reported on its PPP forgiveness application.

That maximization preserves a larger portion of qualified wages to plug into the ERC formulas.

Mortgage Interest Costs

Mortgage interest costs produce PPP loan forgiveness, which the application form instructions describe as follows:[68]

> *(a) covered mortgage obligations: payments of mortgage interest (not including any prepayment or payment of principal) on any business mortgage obligation on real or personal property incurred before February 15, 2020 ("business mortgage interest payments")*

However, a limit rule exists.[69] The forgivable mortgage interest

> *is limited to percent share of the fair market value of the space that is not leased out to a tenant or subtenant.*

---

[68] The loan forgiveness application instructions should be available here: https://home.treasury.gov/system/files/136/PPP-Loan-Forgiveness-Application-Instructions_1_0.pdf

[69] See August 24, 2020 interim final rule Example 2 here: https://home.treasury.gov/system/files/136/PPP--IFR--Treatment-Owners-Forgiveness-Certain-Nonpayroll-Costs.pdf

Accordingly, if a borrower rents 25 percent of a property financed with a mortgage to someone else, only 75 percent of the mortgage interest counts towards forgiveness.

The PPP Loan Forgiveness FAQ says that interest on a refinanced mortgage counts if the original mortgage existed prior to February 15, 2020.[70]

In an interim final rule,[71] the Small Business Administration provided two examples of forgivable mortgage interest costs stemming from a "mortgage" on real or personal property:

> ...the interest on your mortgage for the warehouse you purchased to store business equipment or the interest on an auto loan for a vehicle you use to perform your business...

Describing an auto loan as a "mortgage" seems a stretch.[72] But essentially the Small Business Administration rules seem to say that *any* secured, mortgage-y loan used to buy tangible property—real or personal—potentially creates forgivable "mortgage interest costs."

---

[70] See page 7 here: **https://home.treasury.gov/system/files/136/PPP--Loan-Forgiveness-FAQs.pdf**

[71] See the Interim Final Rule on Additional Eligibility Criteria and Requirements for Certain Pledges of Loans, available here at the time I'm writing this: **https://home.treasury.gov/system/files/136/Interim-Final-Rule-Additional-Eligibility-Criteria-and-Requirements-for-Certain-Pledges-of-Loans.pdf**

[72] Google, for what it's worth, defines a mortgage this way: "a legal agreement by which a bank or other creditor lends money at interest in exchange for taking title of the debtor's property, with the condition that the conveyance of title becomes void upon the payment of the debt."

> *Example 46.* Garfield, Arthur, and Cleveland start a logistics company and borrow money using three separate mortgage loans to buy a warehouse, some machinery, and delivery trucks. A building, the machinery, and truck all count as real or personal property. The interest on all three mortgage loans counts as forgivable mortgage interest if the three partners incurred the loans before February 15, 2020.

The interim final rules and the loan forgiveness applications' instructions provide no specific guidance on loans that aren't secured by a "mortgage," but the PPP Loan Forgiveness FAQ suggests interest on a secured loan is forgivable.[73]

> *Example 47.* Garfield, Arthur, and Cleveland also used a secured credit line to buy forklifts. Further, the credit line agreement gets renewed at the start of every calendar year and it includes a vague collateralization arrangement. Though the lender doesn't actually hold a title interest in the forklifts, the interest costs on the secured credit line apparently count toward PPP forgiveness.

Rent Costs

The loan forgiveness application instructions describe forgivable rent costs as follows:

> *(b) covered rent obligations: business rent or lease payments pursuant to lease agreements for real or personal property in force before February 15, 2020 ("business rent or lease payments")*

---

[73] See Question 4 on page 7 of the PPP Loan Forgiveness FAQ, available here: **https://home.treasury.gov/system/files/136/PPP--Loan-Forgiveness-FAQs.pdf**

As with mortgages, a pro rata limit rule exists.[74] If a borrower leases out 25 percent of a property to someone else, for example, only 75 percent of the rent counts towards forgiveness.

The PPP Loan Forgiveness FAQ says that rent or lease payments on a renewed rental or lease agreement count if the original agreement existed prior to February 15, 2020.[75]

In an interim final rule,[76] the Small Business Administration provides examples of forgivable business rent costs:

> ...the warehouse where you store business equipment or the vehicle you use to perform your business...

These examples of forgivable business rent for tangible property (a building and a vehicle) suggest that forgivable business rent doesn't include amounts paid for intangible property (a software license) but see the later discussion of covered operations expenditures.

---

[74] See August 24, 2020 interim final rule Example 1 here: https://home.treasury.gov/system/files/136/PPP--IFR--Treatment-Owners-Forgiveness-Certain-Nonpayroll-Costs.pdf

[75] See page 7 here: https://home.treasury.gov/system/files/136/PPP--Loan-Forgiveness-FAQs.pdf

[76] See the Interim Final Rule on Additional Eligibility Criteria and Requirements for Certain Pledges of Loans, available here at the time I'm writing this: https://home.treasury.gov/system/files/136/Interim-Final-Rule-Additional-Eligibility-Criteria-and-Requirements-for-Certain-Pledges-of-Loans.pdf

> *Example 48.* Ellen rents offices for her marketing firm and leases both a giant photocopier and a jet. (Don't ask. Long story.) The rent or lease payments on all three items—the office, the photocopier, and the jet—count toward forgiveness if the rent or lease agreement exists prior to February 15, 2020. It turns out that Ellen signed both the office and jet lease agreement in 2019, which means those two rent or lease costs count toward forgiveness. The photocopier lease, unfortunately, she signed on March 1, 2020, which means it doesn't count.

The SBA's interim final rules and loan forgiveness application instructions don't specify how to account for extra costs that appear on a lessor's invoice or landlord's statement. For example, a net lease on industrial space might specify a rent cost and then additional cost reimbursement amounts for property taxes, maintenance, and insurance. Probably borrowers should plan as if those extra costs do not produce forgiveness. But a borrower may want to include these related costs and then just explicitly document their accounting.

> *Example 49.* William and Ida rent industrial space on a net lease. The actual rent equals $1,000 a month. The landlord also collects another $500 a month to reimburse the landlord for property taxes, insurance, and maintenance. William and Ida may want to ask their PPP lender for more detail, but the current SBA guidance suggests they should request forgiveness only for the $1,000 of actual rent.

Self-Rental Costs

The forgiveness rules limit the self-rental costs counted for forgiveness. Specifically, in situations where common ownership between the business and the property owner occurs, the forgivable self-rental costs equal the mortgage interest accrued during the covered period.[77]

Utilities Costs

The loan forgiveness application instructions describe forgivable utilities costs as follows:

> *(c) covered utility payments: business payments for a service for the distribution of electricity, gas, water, telephone, transportation, or internet access for which service began before February 15, 2020 ("business utility payments").*

If a borrower shares utility services with someone, the borrower must prorate utility costs in the same manner as shown on the 2019 tax return or on the expected 2020 tax return.

The Interim Final Rule on Additional Eligibility Criteria and Requirements for Certain Pledges of Loans[78] provides two examples of forgivable business utility costs:

---

[77] See the August 24, 2020 interim final rule's question and answer, "Are rent payments to a related party eligible for forgiveness?", which appears here: **https://home.treasury.gov/system/files/136/PPP--IFR--Treatment-Owners-Forgiveness-Certain-Nonpayroll-Costs.pdf**

[78] See the Interim Final Rule on Additional Eligibility Criteria and Requirements for Certain Pledges of Loans, available here at the time I'm writing this: **https://home.treasury.gov/system/files/136/Interim-Final-Rule-Additional-Eligibility-Criteria-and-Requirements-for-Certain-Pledges-**

> *...the cost of electricity in the warehouse you rent or gas you use driving your business vehicle...*

The SBA's labeling of gas for a vehicle as "utilities" seems odd. But as noted in earlier discussions, regularly the SBA defines terms from the statutes in a way generous to PPP loan borrowers. That said, probably borrowers want to plan conservatively in terms of which utilities costs lead to forgiveness.

> *Example 50.* William and Ida, introduced in the preceding example, also pay electricity, natural gas, water, telephone, and broadband internet bills each month under long-standing service agreements that go back decades. These utility costs surely lead to forgiveness assuming appropriate documentation and then that the costs total less than 40 percent of forgiveness.

Further, the PPP Loan Forgiveness FAQ says that borrowers don't need to "break out" possibly non-utility costs that appear on a utility bill. Charges for things like gross receipts taxes, distribution or supply charges all count as part of the utility cost.[79]

However, though the SBA demonstrates expansive definitions in many locations, a borrower may want to plan conservatively for utility-ish costs that are not specifically labeled as such in guidance from the Small Business Administration.

---

of-Loans.pdf

[79] See Question 7 answer on page 7 available here: https://home.treasury.gov/system/files/136/PPP--Loan-Forgiveness-FAQs.pdf

> *Example 51.* Ida also pays a monthly fee for recycling and garbage service. Garbage is sort of a utility. And she's had this service for years—so before the February 15, 2020 eligibility date. However, because it's not specifically called out as a utility, she may not want to plan on this spending leading to forgiveness.

Home Office Expenses

Home office expenses count toward forgiveness.[80] The forgivable amount, however, gets limited to the percent share deducted on the borrower's 2019 tax return or, for a new business, on the borrower's 2020 tax return.

A borrower who deducts 10 percent of the mortgage interest or rent as home office expenses on her or his 2019 tax return, for example, receives forgiveness only for 10 percent of the mortgage interest or rent paid or incurred during the covered period.

Operations Expenditures

Covered operations expenditures potentially count as spending that can result in PPP loan forgiveness. This grab bag of operating costs includes technology, human resources and accounting costs, including:[81]

---

[80] See August 24, 2020 interim final rule here: **https://home.treasury.gov/system/files/136/PPP--IFR--Treatment-Owners-Forgiveness-Certain-Nonpayroll-Costs.pdf**

[81] Section 101, Continuing Small Business Recovery and Paycheck Protection Program Act.

> ...payment for any business software or cloud computing service that facilitates business operations, product or service delivery, the processing, payment, or tracking of payroll expenses, human resources, sales and billing functions, or accounting tracking of supplies, inventory, records and expenses

Property Damage Costs

Property damage costs represent potential forgivable spending in some cases. The statute describes eligible property damage costs this way:[82]

> a cost related to property damage and vandalism or looting due to public disturbances that occurred during 2020 that was not covered by insurance or other compensation

Supplier Costs

"Covered supplier costs," by which Congress refers to supplies essential to a borrower's operations and provided under a pre-existing contract, also potentially lead to PPP loan forgiveness. The statute provides this definition:

> an expenditure made by an entity to a supplier of goods pursuant to a contract in effect before February 15, 2020 for the supply of goods that are essential to the operations of the entity at the time at which the expenditure is made

---

[82] Ibid.

Worker Protection Expenditures

PPP forgiveness rules also identify worker protection expenditures as spending that may lead to forgiveness. In this category, a borrower includes amounts spent for personal protective equipment and what Congress labeled "adaptive investments."

Employers looking to salvage every dollar of qualified wages they can, probably benefit from having the actual statutory language — even if the language is dense:[83]

> *(9) the term 'covered worker protection expenditure' —*
>
> *(A) means an operating or a capital expenditure that is required to facilitate the adaptation of the business activities of an entity to comply with requirements established or guidance issued by the Department of Health and Human Services, the Centers for Disease Control, or the Occupational Safety and Health Administration during the period beginning on March 1, 2020 and ending December 31, 2020 related to the maintenance of standards for sanitation, social distancing, or any other worker or customer safety requirement related to COVID–19;*
>
> *(B) may include —*
>
> *(i) the purchase, maintenance, or renovation of assets that create or expand —*
>
> *(I) a drive-through window facility;*

---

[83] Ibid

(II) an indoor, outdoor, or combined air or air pressure ventilation or filtration system;

(III) a physical barrier such as a sneeze guard;

(IV) an indoor, outdoor, or combined commercial real property;

(V) an onsite or offsite health screening capability; or

(VI) other assets relating to the compliance with the requirements or guidance described in subparagraph (A), as determined by the Administrator in consultation with the Secretary of Health and Human Services and the Secretary of Labor; and

(ii) the purchase of —

(I) covered materials described in section 328.103(a) of title 44, Code of Federal Regulations, or any successor regulation;

(II) particulate filtering face piece respirators approved by the National Institute for Occupational Safety and Health, including those approved only for emergency use authorization; or

(III) other kinds of personal protective equipment, as determined by the Administrator in consultation with the Secretary of Health and Human Services and the Secretary of Labor; and

(C) does not include residential real property or intangible property;

In short, worker protection includes everything you would guess based on federal, state or local public health directives or recommendations. The materials the government said a small business should use? Those costs potentially lead to PPP loan forgiveness.

Two Tactics to Optimize PPP and ERC

The PPP forgiveness formula results in two basic tactics for maximizing ERC refunds.

First, a PPP borrower wants to base as much forgiveness as possible on nonpayroll costs.

> *Example 52.* An employer who borrowed $162,500 of PPP loan funds and may use up to $65,000 of nonpayroll costs as the basis for PPP loan forgiveness. If the borrower does that, she, he or they only need to show another $97,500 of payroll costs on the PPP forgiveness application in order to secure full forgiveness.

Second an employer wants to get as much PPP payroll costs as possible using spending that counts for PPP payroll costs but not for ERC qualified wages.

> *Example 53.* An employer with a $162,500 PPP loan and $65,000 of forgivable nonpayroll costs still needs another $97,500 of payroll costs for full forgiveness. But if it can get forgiveness for payroll costs that work for PPP forgiveness, but which don't work as qualified wages, it maximizes its ERC. For example, assume that one of the firm's employees is a family member related to the owner who earned wages of $46,154 during the covered period. Further assumed that the owner received compensation during this interval equal to $20,833. And assume that the firm also paid $7,500 of retirement plan expenses and $2,500 of state and local payroll taxes. All of these amounts—so nearly $77,000—lead to PPP loan forgiveness. But using payroll costs that can't be plugged into the ERC formula in this situation, almost eighty percent of the payroll costs represent amounts that are not ERC qualified wages.

Probably some wages needed for PPP forgiveness will "use up" qualified wages that would otherwise plug into ERC formulas. (In the preceding example, the employer still needs about $20,000 of wages, roughly.) But careful allocations of payroll costs on the PPP forgiveness application can save thousands or tens of thousands of dollars of ERC refunds.

IRS Guidance on PPP Wages

In IRS Notice 2021-49, the IRS provides detailed guidance about how to determine which wages an employer elects not to count for ERC purposes because they've elected to use the wages for PPP forgiveness. Sometimes, perhaps, without even realizing these elections were made.

The guidance starts by making this helpful, highly beneficial rule:

> *Specifically, the amount for which the eligible employer is deemed to have made the election is the amount of qualified wages included in the payroll costs reported on the PPP Loan Forgiveness Application up to (but not exceeding) the minimum amount of payroll costs, together with any other eligible expenses reported on the PPP Loan Forgiveness Application, sufficient to support the amount of the PPP loan that is forgiven.*

But this unfortunate reality. The very first example the IRS gives of how the PPP and the ERC interact describes a situation where a borrower uses only wages for its forgiveness application—even though it presumably could have also used other costs. And in this situation, the PPP borrower essentially destroys her, his or their ability to claim ERC refunds based on credits that look at those wages.[84]

Another unfortunate reality to know: If a borrower has already applied for forgiveness, it can't undo that application. Another helpful clarification:

> *An eligible employer is not deemed to have made an election for any qualified wages paid by the eligible employer that are not included in the payroll costs reported on the PPP Loan Forgiveness Application.*

Some examples quoted directly from IRS Notice 2021-20 show how the way the forgiveness application gets filled out affects the leftover qualified wages for ERC.

---

[84] See Example 1 on page 75 of IRS Notice 2021-20

Here's an example where an employer smartly uses nonpayroll costs to protect qualified wages:

> *Employer C submitted a PPP Loan Forgiveness Application and reported the $200,000 of qualified wages as payroll costs, as well as the $70,000 of other eligible expenses, in support of forgiveness of the PPP loan ... In this case, Employer C is deemed to have made an election not to take into account $130,000 of qualified wages for purposes of the employee retention credit, which was the amount of qualified wages included in the payroll costs reported on the PPP Loan Forgiveness Application up to (but not exceeding) the minimum amount of payroll costs, together with the $70,000 of other eligible expenses reported on the PPP Loan Forgiveness Application, sufficient to support the amount of the PPP loan that was forgiven. As a result, $70,000 of the qualified wages reported as payroll costs may be treated as qualified wages for purposes of the employee retention credit.*

Another example shows how things work if the PPP loan borrower reports more payroll costs that are needed:

> *Same facts as [previous example] except Employer C paid $90,000 of other eligible expenses, and reported the $200,000 of qualified wages as payroll costs, as well as the $90,000 of other eligible expenses, in support of forgiveness of the entire PPP loan. In this case, Employer C is deemed to have made an election not to take into account $120,000 of qualified wages for purposes of the employee retention credit, which was the amount of qualified wages included in the payroll costs reported on the PPP Loan Forgiveness Application up to (but not exceeding) the minimum amount of payroll costs, together with the $90,000 of other eligible expenses reported on the PPP Loan Forgiveness Application, sufficient to support the amount of the PPP loan that was forgiven. As a result, $80,000 of the qualified wages reported as payroll costs may be treated as qualified wages for purposes of the employee retention credit.*

And then one other useful example (slightly condensed through editing) where the PPP loan borrower cleverly uses payroll costs for PPP forgiveness that don't work as qualified wages for ERC:

> *Employer D received a PPP loan of $200,000. Employer D is an eligible employer and paid $150,000 of qualified wages that would qualify for the employee retention credit during the second and third quarters of 2020. In addition to the qualified wages, Employer D had $100,000 of other payroll costs that are not qualified wages and $70,000 of other eligible expenses. In order to receive forgiveness of the PPP loan in its entirety, Employer D was required, under the SBA rules, to report $200,000 of payroll costs and other eligible expenses (and a minimum of $120,000 of payroll costs). Employer D submitted a PPP Loan Forgiveness Application and reported $130,000 of payroll costs and $70,000 of other eligible expenses, in support of forgiveness of the entire PPP loan. Employer D can demonstrate that the payroll costs reported on the PPP Loan Forgiveness Application consist of $100,000 of payroll costs that are not qualified wages and $30,000 of payroll costs that are qualified wages… Employer D is deemed to have made an election not to take into account $30,000 of qualified wages for purposes of the employee retention credit… It may not treat that amount as qualified wages for purposes of the employee retention credit. Employer D is not deemed to have made an election with respect to the $120,000 of qualified wages that are not included in the payroll costs reported on the PPP Loan Forgiveness Application.*

Finally, the key thing to note from the example:

> *Accordingly, Employer D may take into account the $120,000 of qualified wages ($150,000 of qualified wages paid minus $30,000 of qualified wages included in the payroll costs reported on the PPP Loan Forgiveness Application) for purposes of the employee retention credit.*

PPP Forgiveness vs ERC

Two closing comments about balancing PPP forgiveness with ERC refund claims.

First, if you have (say) $10,000 of wages in some quarter, that $10,000 might, result in a $7,000 ERC refund. But those $10,000 of wages, if they can be used on a PPP forgiveness application, will produce at least $10,000 of PPP forgiveness. And probably a lot more.

As mentioned in the earlier paragraphs of this chapter, PPP forgiveness stems not just from wages that would be qualified wages for ERC purposes and not just from allocable qualified health plan expenses. PPP forgiveness stems from other fringe benefits (like retirement plans), from state and local payroll taxes, and then from a bunch of other operating costs that—if you have payroll costs—for which you also get forgiveness.

It's very possible, in other words, for $10,000 of qualified wages to produce either a $7,000 ERC refund or nearly $20,000 of PPP forgiveness.

And then here's the main point: If you must choose between ERC and PPP, you would choose PPP. A borrower choosing between $20,000 of forgiveness and a $7,000 ERC refund should choose the $20,000 of forgiveness.

One related comment. The above logic doesn't change if you look at a different year or you consider multiple quarters.

Obviously, if you have an employee who earns $10,000 for two quarters in a row in 2021, so $20,000 in wages, that might absolute best case, result in two $7,000 ERC refunds. Or $14,000 in total ERC money. But $20,000 of qualified wages for ERC purposes would mean at least, bare minimum, $20,000 of PPP forgiveness. And of course, that $20,000 of ERC qualified wages probably grows to close to $40,000 of PPP forgivable payroll and non-payroll costs

A final comment to make here: Many PPP borrowers completed and submitted PPP forgiveness applications before the PPP and ERC laws allowed an employer to both claim ERC refunds and receive PPP loan forgiveness.[85] A good chance exists for first draw PPP loan borrowers that an employer shouldn't even have thought about ERC and PPP together.

---

[85] The Consolidated Appropriations Act (2021), relevant portions of which are reproduced as Appendix B, made this change.

Chapter 7: Tax Accounting for ERC Transactions

This very short chapter quickly describes the tax accounting ERC eligible employers need to use.

The Basic Rule: Adjust Deductions for Credits

The basic rule works like this: An eligible employer must adjust its wage and qualified health plan deductions for the employee retention credits it claims. That adjustment occurs on the income tax return that reports the wages.[86]

> *Example 54.* In mid-2021, an employer amended its 2020 941 quarterly payroll tax returns to claim $50,000 of retention credits for the third and fourth quarter of 2020. If the employer has not yet filed its 2020 tax return, it should do so, reducing downward the wages and qualified health plan deductions by $50,000.

If an employer already filed its 2020 tax return and then sometime later files for ERC refunds, it should amend the original income tax return filed for 2020.

---

[86] Section 2301(e) sets this requirement, saying "rules similar to section 280C(a) of the Code apply for purposes of the employee retention credit."

> *Example 55.* In mid-2021, a different employer also amended its 2020 941 quarterly payroll tax returns to claim $50,000 of retention credits for the third and fourth quarter of 2020. This employer had already filed its 2020 income tax return before it amended its 941 payroll tax returns. This employer should amend its original 2020 income tax return, in the process removing $50,000 of wages and qualified health plan deductions.

Mismatched Deductions and Credits

Just to clear up a point of possible confusion, the timing of the actual refund doesn't matter in terms of on which return an employer shows the credit adjustment.

> *Example 56.* An employer files a quarterly 941-X refund claim for the second and third quarter of 2020. As the year 2021 ends, unfortunately, the employer has still not received the refunds on the claims now filed months earlier. But that doesn't matter. The employer should still amend its 2020 income tax return. Even if it may need the ERC refund to pay for the income taxes triggered by the adjustment.

Example ERC Bookkeeping Transactions

The bookkeeping for ERC transactions should be easy and straightforward.

Journal Entry When Amending 941 Return

To record a refund claim based on a quarter in a previous year, one easy approach might be to first record a journal for the quarter to which the refund claim connects.

A $10,000 refund claim, for example, might be recorded as follows:

	Debit	Credit
Wages Expense		$10,000
ERC Refund Receivable	$10,000	

That credit to wages expense reduces the deduction. The debit shows the amount the IRS owes the employer. The journal entry date would be in the tax year that shows the deductions for the wages that produce the ERC. If an employer were amending a 941 payroll returns for 2020 to claim a refund, the date of the journal entry like the one just shown might be 12/31/2020.

When the employer receives the ERC refund, the obvious journal entry probably looks like this:

	Debit	Credit
Bank Account	$10,000	
ERC Refund Receivable		$10,000

The date for the above journal entry? Probably the date the employer receives the refund check.

The one other thing to check — and this probably depends on the accounting software used — is this: The $10,000 credit that reduces the wages expenses should appear in same tax year as the wages from which the credit stems.

Journal Entry When Refund on Original 941

In the simpler situation where the ERC refund claim is made in the current quarter, the usual accounting may automatically reflect what's going on.

If the payroll system simply pulls $10,000 less money out of the bank account, buried in the usual payroll transactions may be a $10,000 reduction in the wages deduction and a $10,000 reduction in the cash used for payroll.

In effect, the following journal entry has been appended to the usual payroll journal entry:

	Debit	Credit
Wages Expense		$10,000
Bank Account	$10,000	

Chapter 8: Tips for Maximizing ERC Refunds

This book ends with a laundry list of tips and tricks for maximizing an employer's employee retention credits.

The tips and tricks that follow repeat, echo or amplify information provided in earlier chapters. But that's probably okay. The employee retention credit burdens taxpayers with surprising complexity.

Reviewing the tax-saving opportunities available one last time—just to make sure an employer doesn't miss savings—makes good sense.

Tip #1: Use Eligibility Based on Gross Receipts

The first and easiest-to-use tip: Check to see if you or your client qualify for ERC eligibility based on a substantial decline in gross receipts.

For 2020, a substantial decline in gross receipts means more than a fifty percent reduction as compared to the same quarter in 2019. But an employer continues to be eligible in 2020 until the quarter after its revenues exceed eighty percent of the gross receipts for the same quarter in 2019.

For 2021, a substantial decline means more than a twenty percent reduction for a quarter.

Basing ERC eligibility status on a substantial reduction in gross receipts is easy. You only need to keep your accounting records up to date

Furthermore, you can often simply "tell" your payroll service that you are eligible and they'll correctly reflect the ERC on your quarterly 941 payroll tax returns.

Tip #2: Look at 2020 If Employer Started in 2019

If an employer started operations during 2019 and so wasn't operating some quarter, you can compare 2021 quarterly revenues to 2020 quarterly revenues. (Chapter 2, "Eligible Employers," explains how and when to do this.)

Tip #3: Consider the Alternative Quarter Method

If an employer can't achieve eligibility by comparing a quarter to the same quarter from 2019 or 2020, it should see if it can use the "Alternative Quarter" method.

As discussed in Chapter 2, "Eligible Employers," with the alternative quarter method, to determine eligibility for a current quarter in 2021, an employer compares its gross receipts for the immediately preceding quarter to the corresponding quarter in 2019 (or in 2020 if the employer didn't exist for that quarter of 2019).

Using the alternative quarter method may allow an employer to achieve the relatively easy and straightforward eligibility provided by a comparison of quarterly gross receipts.

Tip #4: Expand the Interval of Eligibility

An employer may be able to create eligibility by identifying periods when it suffers either full suspension or partial suspension.

For example, an employer that qualifies for ERC eligibility in the third and fourth quarter of 2020 based on a substantial decline in gross revenues—so from July 1 through December 31—may increase the window of eligibility if it can determine and then document it was fully or partially suspended for the month of June. Or the first two weeks of January 2021.

Tip #5: Verify Your Local Non-profit Knows

Do you have a local charity you support and volunteer in? A house of worship you attend?

Make sure the leadership group or management team there know their tax-exempt organization potentially qualifies for ERC refunds.

This same expansive eligibility applies to tribes and tribal entities, too.

Tip #6: Acquire Another Trade or Business

The aggregation rules described in Chapter 5, "How Aggregation Works," can both hinder and help an employer trying to claim ERC.

For example, the aggregation rules may cause an employer to be treated as a large eligible employer, which means (potentially) the employer calculates more modest qualified wages amounts.

But the aggregation rules can also result in an employer qualifying too. A small eligible employer that aggregates two trades or businesses may get enjoy full ERC eligibility if one of the trades or businesses is suspended.

Aggregation may therefore provide a way for an employer to sculpt its financial features in a way that results in ERC eligibility.

Tip #7: Use Nonpayroll Costs for PPP Forgiveness

As noted in Chapter 6, "Balancing ERC and PPP," wages used on a PPP forgiveness application can't be recycled and plugged into an ERC formula.

Accordingly, one hugely impactful thing that some PPP borrowers can do to boost their ERC qualified wages? Report more nonpayroll costs on the forgiveness application.

That results in the employer reporting less wages on the application. Which means, probably, more wages left over for purposes of ERC calculations.

Chapter 6 discusses this approach and provides what amounts to an IRS-approved method to maximize ERC by boosting qualified wages.

Tip #8: Maximize Owner and Family Wages

Another tip related to the PPP loans? Owner compensation and then the wages of the owner's family often work for PPP forgiveness but not for ERC refunds.

If a PPP borrower has not yet applied for forgiveness, therefore, the owners really want to report as much owner and family member wages on the PPP forgiveness application as possible.

Tip #9: Use a 24-week Covered Period

One final tip related to PPP loans and their impact on ERC refunds.

A PPP borrower can look at either payroll and nonpayroll spending over eight weeks or over 24-weeks. Because a 24-week interval captures a larger chunk of nonpayroll costs, and also payroll related costs that work for PPP forgiveness but not for ERC, probably PPP borrowers who want to maximize the ERCs should use a 24-week covered period.

Tip #10: Start a Recovery Start-up Business

If an employer's average gross receipts for three preceding tax years average $1 million or less annually, and the employer doesn't already qualify for ERC in the third and fourth quarters of 2021, it may want to consider starting a new trade or business. (The new trade or business needs to start after February 15, 2020 as discussed in Chapter 4, "Startup Trades and Businesses.")

Starting that new trade or business can qualify an employer not otherwise beat up by the COVID-19 pandemic with up to a $50,000 per quarter ERC.

For example, a restaurant that starts a retail business should generate ERC refunds for both the restaurant's employees and for the retail business's eligible employers.

Tip #11: Start a New Trade or Business ASAP

Finally, a tip related to starting a new trade or business in order to get an ERC.

Technically, you only need to start the new trade or business by the end of the quarter in order to qualify for ERC for the quarter. Starting a business on the last day of September, for example, qualifies you for ERC for the third quarter. (That quarter ends on September 30, obviously.)

I think you want to start as early as you can. The earlier you start, the more evidence you create that you have started the new trade or business. The earlier you start, the more likely it becomes, at least in my mind, that everything that needs to be up and running is, in fact, up and running.

To borrow an analogy from the game of football, a touchdown occurs when the football crosses that plane that separates the playing field from the endzone. But sometimes, officials and fans need an instant replay camera and careful analysis to determine if "the ball *really* broke the plane."

Situations, in comparison, where some runner or receiver carries the ball several steps into or catches the ball deep inside the endzone? Clear cut. No need for an instant replay or extended discussions.

You want, I argue, a clear cut, obvious starting point.

Glossary of Terms

941: The quarterly payroll tax return employers file to report the wages paid, federal income taxes withheld, and then Social Security and Medicare taxes owed. The ERC goes on this form.

941-X: The quarterly payroll tax return employers file to amend a previously filed Form 941. A refund claim based on the ERC for some past quarter goes on this form.

aggregation: Combining the full-time employees, gross receipts and qualified wages, and suspensions for employers with the roughly same ownership into a single employer for purposes of the employee retention credit formulas.

allocable health plan expenses: Health plan expenses paid or incurred by an employer to provide and maintain a group health plan, but only to the extent such amounts are excluded from the gross income of employees by reason of Section 106(a) of the tax code

covered period: The interval of time during which PPP loan funds get spent on payroll and nonpayroll costs. Usually 24 weeks.

disqualified wages: Wages which don't lead to an employee retention credit. Wages paid to a majority business owner and the family members of a majority business owner usually fall into this category.

eligible employer: An employer eligible for claiming employee retention credits due to a substantial decline in gross receipts, a government order suspending its operations, or starting a new trade or business.

employer retention credit (ERC): A reduction in the payroll tax deposit required on an employer's quarterly 941 payroll tax return. The credit equals fifty percent of the first $10,000 an employee earns in 2020 (so a maximum of $5,000 per employee for the year). The credit equals seventy percent of the first $10,000 an employee earns in a quarter in 2021 (so $7,000 per employee per quarter and as much as $28,000 for the year).

full suspension: When a government order limiting commerce, travel, or group meetings (for commercial, social, religious, or other purposes) due to COVID-19 causes an employer to totally suspend operations.

full-time employee: An employee who on average worked thirty or more hours each week in the 2019 or 2020.

government orders: Orders, proclamations, or decrees from the Federal or any state or local government that limit "commerce, travel, or group meetings (for commercial, social, religious, or other purposes) due to the coronavirus disease 2019 (COVID-19)."

gross receipts: Total revenues, investment income and other income an employer receives. For purposes of ERC, includes PPP forgiveness at the option of the employer.

health plan expenses: See allocable health plan expenses

large eligible employer: For 2020 ERC calculations, an employer that employed more than 100 full-time employees in 2019. For 2021 ERC calculations, an employer that employed more than 500 full-time employees in 2019.

partial suspension: When a government order limiting commerce, travel, or group meetings (for commercial, social, religious, or other purposes) due to COVID-19 causes an employer to suspend a part of the operation that represents ten percent or more of gross receipts or hours or service.

Paycheck Protection Program (PPP): An SBA loan program that provided either two and half months or three and half moneys of average monthly payroll costs for employers facing economic uncertainty due to COVID-19. The loans were fully forgivable as long as the borrower spent the money in specified ways. Wages paid with PPP funds can't be used for ERC.

qualified wages: The employee wages an employer may use for purposes of calculating the employee retention credit. Not all wages lead to an employee retention credit.

recovery startup business: An employer who begins carrying on a trade or business sometime after February 15, 2020 if the employer's average gross receipts average not more than $1,000,000 for the three previous tax years.

severely financially distressed employer: An eligible employer with gross receipts that are less than 10 percent of the gross receipts for the same calendar quarter in calendar year 2019 (or 2020.) A severely financially distressed large eligible employer counts all the wages its pays as qualified wages—not just the wages it pays to employees not providing services.

small eligible employer: For 2020 ERC calculations, an employer that employed 100 or fewer full-time employees in 2019. For 2021 ERC calculations, an employer that employed 500 or fewer full-time employees in 2019.

trade or business: An activity a taxpayer engages in for income or profit and with regularity and continuity.

wages: Amounts employers pay employees for their work

Appendix A: Section 2301

Coronavirus Aid, Relief, and Economic Security Act, Public Law 136, 116th Cong., 2nd sess. (27 March 2020), sec. 2301

SEC. 2301. EMPLOYEE RETENTION CREDIT FOR EMPLOYERS SUBJECT TO CLOSURE DUE TO COVID-19.

(a) IN GENERAL.—In the case of an eligible employer, there shall be allowed as a credit against applicable employment taxes for each calendar quarter an amount equal to 50 percent of the qualified wages with respect to each employee of such employer for such calendar quarter.

(b) LIMITATIONS AND REFUNDABILITY.—

(1) WAGES TAKEN INTO ACCOUNT.—The amount of qualified wages with respect to any employee which may be taken into account under subsection (a) by the eligible employer for all calendar quarters shall not exceed $10,000.

(2) CREDIT LIMITED TO EMPLOYMENT TAXES.—The credit allowed by subsection (a) with respect to any calendar quarter shall not exceed the applicable employment taxes (reduced by any credits allowed under subsections (e) and (f) of section 3111 of the Internal Revenue Code of 1986 and sections 7001 and 7003 of the Families First Coronavirus Response Act) on the wages paid with respect to the employment of all the employees of the eligible employer for such calendar quarter.

(3) REFUNDABILITY OF EXCESS CREDIT.—

(A) IN GENERAL.—If the amount of the credit under subsection (a) exceeds the limitation of paragraph (2) for any calendar quarter, such excess shall be treated as an overpayment that shall be refunded under sections 6402(a) and 6413(b) of the Internal Revenue Code of 1986.

(B) TREATMENT OF PAYMENTS.—For purposes of section 1324 of title 31, United States Code, any amounts due to the employer under this paragraph shall be treated in the same manner as a refund due from a credit provision referred to in subsection (b)(2) of such section.

(c) DEFINITIONS.—For purposes of this section—

(1) APPLICABLE EMPLOYMENT TAXES.—The term "applicable employment taxes" means the following:

(A) The taxes imposed under section 3111(a) of the Internal Revenue Code of 1986.

(B) So much of the taxes imposed under section 3221(a) of such Code as are attributable to the rate in effect under section 3111(a) of such Code.

(2) ELIGIBLE EMPLOYER.—

(A) IN GENERAL.—The term "eligible employer" means any employer—

(i) which was carrying on a trade or business during calendar year 2020, and

(ii) with respect to any calendar quarter, for which—

(I) the operation of the trade or business described in clause (i) is fully or partially suspended during the calendar quarter due to orders from an appropriate governmental authority limiting commerce, travel, or group meetings (for commercial, social, religious, or other purposes) due to the coronavirus disease 2019 (COVID–19), or

(II) such calendar quarter is within the period described in subparagraph (B).

(B) SIGNIFICANT DECLINE IN GROSS RECEIPTS.—The period described in this subparagraph is the period—

(i) beginning with the first calendar quarter beginning after December 31, 2019, for which gross receipts (within the meaning of section 448(c) of the Internal Revenue Code of 1986) for the calendar quarter are less than 50 percent of gross receipts for the same calendar quarter in the prior year, and

(ii) ending with the calendar quarter following the first calendar quarter beginning after a calendar quarter described in clause (i) for which gross receipts of such employer are greater than 80 percent of gross receipts for the same calendar quarter in the prior year.

(C) TAX-EXEMPT ORGANIZATIONS.—In the case of an organization which is described in section 501(c) of the Internal Revenue Code of 1986 and exempt from tax under section 501(a) of such Code, clauses (i) and (ii)(I) of subparagraph (A) shall apply to all operations of such organization.

(3) QUALIFIED WAGES.—

(A) IN GENERAL.—The term "qualified wages" means—

(i) in the case of an eligible employer for which the average number of full-time employees (within the meaning of section 4980H of the Internal Revenue Code of 1986) employed by such eligible employer during 2019 was greater than 100, wages paid by such eligible employer with respect to which an employee is not providing services due to circumstances described in subclause (I) or (II) of paragraph (2)(A)(ii), or

(ii) in the case of an eligible employer for which the average number of full-time employees (within the meaning of section 4980H of the Internal Revenue Code of 1986) employed by such eligible employer during 2019 was not greater than 100—

(I) with respect to an eligible employer described in subclause (I) of paragraph (2)(A)(ii), wages paid by such eligible employer with respect to an employee during any period described in such clause, or

(II) with respect to an eligible employer described in subclause (II) of such paragraph, wages paid by such eligible employer with respect to an employee during such quarter. Such term shall not include any wages taken into account under section 7001 or section 7003 of the Families First Coronavirus Response Act.

(B) LIMITATION.—Qualified wages paid or incurred by an eligible employer described in subparagraph (A)(i) with respect to an employee for any period described in such subparagraph may not exceed the amount such employee would have been paid for working an equivalent duration during the 30 days immediately preceding such period.

(C) ALLOWANCE FOR CERTAIN HEALTH PLAN EXPENSES.—

(i) IN GENERAL.—The term "qualified wages" shall include so much of the eligible employer's qualified health plan expenses as are properly allocable to such wages.

(ii) QUALIFIED HEALTH PLAN EXPENSES.—For purposes of this paragraph, the term "qualified health plan expenses" means amounts paid or incurred by the eligible employer to provide and maintain a group health plan (as defined in section 5000(b)(1) of the Internal Revenue Code of 1986), but only to the extent that such amounts are excluded from the gross income of employees by reason of section 106(a) of such Code.

(iii) ALLOCATION RULES.—For purposes of this paragraph, qualified health plan expenses shall be allocated to qualified wages in such manner as the Secretary may prescribe. Except as otherwise provided by the Secretary, such allocation shall be treated as properly made if made on the basis of being pro rata among employees and pro rata on the basis of periods of coverage (relative to the periods to which such wages relate).

(4) SECRETARY.—The term "Secretary" means the Secretary of the Treasury or the Secretary's delegate.

(5) WAGES.—The term "wages" means wages (as defined in section 3121(a) of the Internal Revenue Code of 1986) and compensation (as defined in section 3231(e) of such Code).

(6) OTHER TERMS.—Any term used in this section which is also used in chapter 21 or 22 of the Internal Revenue Code of 1986 shall have the same meaning as when used in such chapter.

(d) AGGREGATION RULE.—All persons treated as a single employer under subsection (a) or (b) of section 52 of the Internal Revenue Code of 1986, or subsection (m) or (o) of section 414 of such Code, shall be treated as one employer for purposes of this section.

(e) CERTAIN RULES TO APPLY.—For purposes of this section, rules similar to the rules of sections 51(i)(1) and 280C(a) of the Internal Revenue Code of 1986 shall apply.

(f) CERTAIN GOVERNMENTAL EMPLOYERS.—This credit shall not apply to the Government of the United States, the government of any State or political subdivision thereof, or any agency or instrumentality of any of the foregoing.

(g) ELECTION NOT TO HAVE SECTION APPLY.—This section shall not apply with respect to any eligible employer for any calendar quarter if such employer elects (at such time and in such manner as the Secretary may prescribe) not to have this section apply.

(h) SPECIAL RULES.—

(1) EMPLOYEE NOT TAKEN INTO ACCOUNT MORE THAN ONCE.—An employee shall not be included for purposes of this section for any period with respect to any employer if such employer is allowed a credit under section 51 of the Internal Revenue Code of 1986 with respect to such employee for such period.

(2) DENIAL OF DOUBLE BENEFIT.—Any wages taken into account in determining the credit allowed under this section shall not be taken into account for purposes of determining the credit allowed under section 45S of such Code.

(3) THIRD PARTY PAYORS.—Any credit allowed under this section shall be treated as a credit described in section 3511(d)(2) of such Code.

(i) TRANSFERS TO FEDERAL OLD-AGE AND SURVIVORS INSURANCE TRUST FUND.—There are hereby appropriated to the Federal OldAge and Survivors Insurance Trust Fund and the Federal Disability Insurance Trust Fund established under section 201 of the Social Security Act (42 U.S.C. 401) and the Social Security Equivalent Benefit Account established under section 15A(a) of the Railroad Retirement Act of 1974 (45 U.S.C. 14 231n–1(a)) amounts equal to the reduction in revenues to the Treasury by reason of this section (without regard to this subsection). Amounts appropriated by the preceding sentence shall be transferred from the general fund at such times and in such manner as to replicate to the extent possible the transfers which would have occurred to such Trust Fund or Account had this section not been enacted.

(j) RULE FOR EMPLOYERS TAKING SMALL BUSINESS INTERRUPTION LOAN.—If an eligible employer receives a covered loan under paragraph (36) of section 7(a) of the Small Business Act (15 U.S.C. 636(a)), as added by section 1102 of this Act, such employer shall not be eligible for the credit under this section.

(k) TREATMENT OF DEPOSITS.—The Secretary shall waive any penalty under section 6656 of the Internal Revenue Code of 1986 for any failure to make a deposit of any applicable employment taxes if the Secretary determines that such failure was due to the reasonable anticipation of the credit allowed under this section.

(l) REGULATIONS AND GUIDANCE.—The Secretary shall issue such forms, instructions, regulations, and guidance as are necessary—

(1) to allow the advance payment of the credit under subsection (a), subject to the limitations provided in this section, based on such information as the Secretary shall require,

(2) to provide for the reconciliation of such advance payment with the amount advanced at the time of filing the return of tax for the applicable calendar quarter or taxable year,

(3) to provide for the recapture of the credit under this section if such credit is allowed to a taxpayer which receives a loan described in subsection (j) during a subsequent quarter,

(4) with respect to the application of the credit under subsection (a) to third party payors (including professional employer organizations, certified professional employer organizations, or agents under section 3504 of the Internal Revenue Code of 1986), including regulations or guidance allowing such payors to submit documentation necessary to substantiate the eligible employer status of employers that use such payors, and

(5) for application of subparagraphs (A)(ii)(II) and (B) of subsection (c)(2) in the case of any employer which was not carrying on a trade or business for all or part of the same calendar quarter in the prior year.

(m) APPLICATION.—This section shall only apply to wages paid after March 12, 2020, and before January 1, 2021.

Appendix B: Sections 206, 207 and 303

Consolidated Appropriations Act, 2021, Public Law 260, 116th Cong., 2nd sess. (27 December 2020), div. EE secs. 206-7, 303

SEC. 206. CLARIFICATIONS AND TECHNICAL IMPROVEMENTS TO CARES ACT EMPLOYEE RETENTION CREDIT. —

(a) GROSS RECEIPTS OF TAX-EXEMPT ORGANIZATIONS.— Section 2301(c)(2)(C) of the CARES Act is amended—
> (1) by striking "of such Code, clauses (i) and (ii)(I)" and inserting "of such Code—
>> "(i) clauses (i) and (ii)(I)",
>
> (2) by striking the period at the end and inserting ", and", and
> (3) by adding at the end the following new clause:
>> "(ii) any reference in this section to gross receipts shall be treated as a reference to gross receipts within the meaning of section 6033 of such Code.".

(b) MODIFICATION OF TREATMENT OF HEALTH PLAN EXPENSES.— Section 2301(c) of the CARES Act is amended—
> (1) by striking subparagraph (C) of paragraph (3), and
> (2) in paragraph (5)—
>> (A) by striking "The term" and inserting the following:
>> "(A) IN GENERAL.—The term", and

(B) by adding at the end the following new subparagraph:

"(B) ALLOWANCE FOR CERTAIN HEALTH PLAN EXPENSES.—

"(i) IN GENERAL.—Such term shall include amounts paid by the eligible employer to provide and maintain a group health plan (as defined in section 5000(b)(1) of the Internal Revenue Code of 1986), but only to the extent that such amounts are excluded from the gross income of employees by reason of section 106(a) of such Code.

"(ii) ALLOCATION RULES.—For purposes of this section, amounts treated as wages under clause (i) shall be treated as paid with respect to any employee (and with respect to any period) to the extent that such amounts are properly allocable to such employee (and to such period) in such manner as the Secretary may prescribe. Except as otherwise provided by the Secretary, such allocation shall be treated as properly made if made on the basis of being pro rata among periods of coverage.".

(c) IMPROVED COORDINATION BETWEEN PAYCHECK PROTECTION PROGRAM AND EMPLOYEE RETENTION TAX CREDIT.—

(1) AMENDMENT TO PAYCHECK PROTECTION PROGRAM.— Section 7A(a)(12) of the Small Business Act, as redesignated, transferred, and amended by the Economic Aid to Hard-Hit Small Businesses, Nonprofits, and Venues Act, is amended by adding at the end the following: "Such payroll costs shall not include qualified wages taken into account in determining the credit allowed under section 2301 of the CARES Act or qualified wages taken into account in determining the credit allowed under subsection (a) or (d) of section 303 of the Taxpayer Certainty and Disaster Relief Act of 2020." .

(2) AMENDMENTS TO EMPLOYEE RETENTION TAX CREDIT.—

    (A) IN GENERAL.— Section 2301(g) of the CARES Act is amended to read as follows:

"(g) ELECTION TO NOT TAKE CERTAIN WAGES INTO ACCOUNT.—

    "(1) IN GENERAL.—This section shall not apply to so much of the qualified wages paid by an eligible employer as such employer elects (at such time and in such manner as the Secretary may prescribe) to not take into account for purposes of this section.

"(2) COORDINATION WITH PAYCHECK PROTECTION PROGRAM.—The Secretary, in consultation with the Administrator of the Small Business Administration, shall issue guidance providing that payroll costs paid during the covered period shall not fail to be treated as qualified wages under this section by reason of an election under paragraph (1) to the extent that a covered loan of the eligible employer is not forgiven by reason of a decision under section 7A(g) of the Small Business Act. Terms used in the preceding sentence which are also used in section 7A of the Small Business Act shall have the same meaning as when used in such section.".

(B) CONFORMING AMENDMENTS.—
    (i) Section 2301 of the CARES Act is amended by striking subsection (j).
    (ii) Section 2301(l) of the CARES Act is amended by striking paragraph (3) and by redesignating paragraphs (4) and (5) as paragraphs (3) and (4), respectively.

(d) REGULATIONS AND GUIDANCE.— Section 2301(l) of the CARES Act, as amended by subsection (c)(2)(B)(ii), is amended by striking "and" at the end of paragraph (3), by striking the period at the end of paragraph (4) and inserting ", and" , and by adding at the end the following new paragraph:
    "(5) to prevent the avoidance of the purposes of the limitations under this section, including through the leaseback of employees.".

(e) EFFECTIVE DATE.—
    (1) IN GENERAL.— The amendments made by this section shall take effect as if included in the provisions of the CARES Act to which they relate.
    (2) SPECIAL RULE.—

(A) IN GENERAL.— For purposes of section 2301 of the CARES Act, an employer who has filed a return of tax with respect to applicable employment taxes (as defined in section 2301(c)(1) of division A of such Act) before the date of the enactment of this Act may elect (in such manner as the Secretary of the Treasury (or the Secretary's delegate) shall prescribe) to treat any applicable amount as an amount paid in the calendar quarter which includes the date of the enactment of this Act.

(B) APPLICABLE AMOUNT.— For purposes of subparagraph (A), the term "applicable amount" means the amount of wages which—

  (i) are—

    (I) described in section 2301(c)(5)(B) of the CARES Act, as added by the amendments made by subsection (b), or

    (II) permitted to be treated as qualified wages under guidance issued pursuant to section 2301(g)(2) of the CARES Act (as added by subsection (c)), and

  (ii) were—

    (I) paid in a calendar quarter beginning after December 31, 2019, and before October 1, 2020, and

  (II) not taken into account by the taxpayer in calculating the credit allowed under section 2301(a) of division A of such Act for such calendar quarter.

SEC. 207. EXTENSION AND MODIFICATION OF EMPLOYEE RETENTION AND REHIRING TAX CREDIT.

(a) EXTENSION.—
   (1) IN GENERAL.— Section 2301(m) of the CARES Act is amended by striking "January 1, 2021" and inserting "July 1, 2021".
   (2) CONFORMING AMENDMENT.— Section 2301(c)(2)(A)(i) of the CARES Act is amended by striking "during calendar year 2020" and inserting "during the calendar quarter for which the credit is determined under subsection (a)".
(b) INCREASE IN CREDIT PERCENTAGE.— Section 2301(a) of the CARES Act is amended by striking "50 percent" and inserting "70 percent".
(c) INCREASE IN PER EMPLOYEE LIMITATION.— Section 2301(b)(1) of the CARES Act is amended by striking "for all calendar quarters shall not exceed $10,000" and inserting "for any calendar quarter shall not exceed $10,000".
(d) MODIFICATIONS TO DEFINITION OF ELIGIBLE EMPLOYER.—
   (1) DECREASE IN REDUCTION IN GROSS RECEIPTS NECESSARY TO QUALIFY AS ELIGIBLE EMPLOYER.—
      (A) IN GENERAL.— Section 2301(c)(2)(A)(ii)(II) of the CARES Act is amended to read as follows:
         "(II) the gross receipts (within the meaning of section 448(c) of the Internal Revenue Code of 1986) of such employer for such calendar quarter are less than 80 percent of the gross receipts of such employer for the same calendar quarter in calendar year 2019.".
      (B) APPLICATION TO EMPLOYERS NOT IN EXISTENCE IN 2019.— Section 2301(c)(2)(A) of the CARES Act, as amended by subparagraph (A), is amended by adding at the end the following new flush sentence:

"With respect to any employer for any calendar quarter, if such employer was not in existence as of the beginning of the same calendar quarter in calendar year 2019, clause (ii)(II) shall be applied by substituting '2020' for '2019'.".

(2) ELECTION TO DETERMINE GROSS RECEIPTS TEST BASED ON PRIOR QUARTER.—

(A) IN GENERAL.— Subparagraph (B) of section 2301(c)(2) of the CARES Act is amended to read as follows:

"(B) ELECTION TO USE ALTERNATIVE QUARTER.—At the election of the employer—

"(i) subparagraph (A)(ii)(II) shall be applied—

"(I) by substituting 'for the immediately preceding calendar quarter' for 'for such calendar quarter', and

"(II) by substituting 'the corresponding calendar quarter in calendar year 2019' for 'the same calendar quarter in calendar year 2019', and

"(ii) the last sentence of subparagraph (A) shall be applied by substituting 'the corresponding calendar quarter in calendar year 2019' for 'the same calendar quarter in calendar year 2019'.

An election under this subparagraph shall be made at such time and in such manner as the Secretary shall prescribe.".

(B) CONFORMING AMENDMENT.— Section 2301(l) of the CARES Act, as amended by section 206, is amended by inserting "and" at the end of paragraph (3), by striking paragraph (4), and by redesignating paragraph (5) as paragraph (4).

(3) APPLICATION TO CERTAIN GOVERNMENTAL EMPLOYERS.—

(A) IN GENERAL.— Section 2301(f) of the CARES Act is amended—

(i) by striking "This" and inserting the following:

"(1) IN GENERAL.—This", and

(ii) by adding at the end the following new paragraph:

"(2) EXCEPTION.—Paragraph (1) shall not apply to—

"(A) any organization described in section 501(c)(1) of the Internal Revenue Code of 1986 and exempt from tax under section 501(a) of such Code, or

"(B) any entity described in paragraph (1) if —

"(i) such entity is a college or university, or

"(ii) the principal purpose or function of such entity is providing medical or hospital care.

In the case of any entity described in subparagraph (B), such entity shall be treated as satisfying the requirements of subsection (c)(2)(A)(i).".

(B) CONFORMING AMENDMENT.— Section 2301(c)(5)(A) of the CARES Act, as amended by section 206(b)(2), is amended by adding at the end the following new sentence:

"For purposes of the preceding sentence, in the case of any organization or entity described in subsection (f)(2), wages as defined in section 3121(a) of the Internal Revenue Code of 1986 shall be determined without regard to paragraphs (5), (6), (7), (10), and (13) of section 3121(b) of such Code (except with respect to services performed in a penal institution by an inmate thereof).".

(e) MODIFICATION OF DETERMINATION OF QUALIFIED WAGES.—

(1) MODIFICATION OF THRESHOLD FOR TREATMENT AS A LARGE EMPLOYER.— Section 2301(c)(3)(A) of the CARES Act is amended by striking "100" each place it appears in clauses (i) and (ii) and inserting "500".

(2) ELIMINATION OF LIMITATION.— Section 2301(c)(3) of the CARES Act is amended—

(A) by striking subparagraph (B), and

(B) by striking "Such term" in the second sentence of subparagraph (A) and inserting the following:

"(B) EXCEPTION.—The term 'qualified wages'".

(f) DENIAL OF DOUBLE BENEFIT.— Section 2301(h) of the CARES Act is amended—

(1) by striking paragraphs (1) and (2) and inserting the following:

"(1) DENIAL OF DOUBLE BENEFIT.—Any wages taken into account in determining the credit allowed under this section shall not be taken into account as wages for purposes of sections 41, 45A, 45P, 45S, 51, and 1396 of the Internal Revenue Code of 1986.".

(2) by redesignating paragraph (3) as paragraph (2).

(g) ADVANCE PAYMENTS.—

(1) IN GENERAL.— Section 2301 of the CARES Act, as amended by section 206(c)(2)(B)(i), is amended by inserting after subsection (i) the following new subsection:

"(j) ADVANCE PAYMENTS.—

"(1) IN GENERAL.—Except as provided in paragraph (2), no advance payment of the credit under subsection (a) shall be allowed.

"(2) ADVANCE PAYMENTS TO SMALL EMPLOYERS.—

"(A) IN GENERAL.—Under rules provided by the Secretary, an eligible employer for which the average number of full-time employees (within the meaning of section 4980H of the Internal Revenue Code of 1986) employed by such eligible employer during 2019 was not greater than 500 may elect for any calendar quarter to receive an advance payment of the credit under subsection (a) for such quarter in an amount not to exceed 70 percent of the average quarterly wages paid by the employer in calendar year 2019.

"(B) SPECIAL RULE FOR SEASONAL EMPLOYERS.—In the case of any employer who employs seasonal workers (as defined in section 45R(d)(5)(B) of the Internal Revenue Code of 1986), the employer may elect to substitute 'the wages for the calendar quarter in 2019 which corresponds to the calendar quarter to which the election relates' for 'the average quarterly wages paid by the employer in calendar year 2019'.

"(C) SPECIAL RULE FOR EMPLOYERS NOT IN EXISTENCE IN 2019.—In the case of any employer that was not in existence in 2019, subparagraphs (A) and (B) shall each be applied by substituting '2020' for '2019' each place it appears.

"(3) RECONCILIATION OF CREDIT WITH ADVANCE PAYMENTS.—

"(A) IN GENERAL.—The amount of credit which would (but for this subsection) be allowed under this section shall be reduced (but not below zero) by the aggregate payment allowed to the taxpayer under paragraph (2). Any failure to so reduce the credit shall be treated as arising out of a mathematical or clerical error and assessed according to section 6213(b)(1) of the Internal Revenue Code of 1986.

"(B) EXCESS ADVANCE PAYMENTS.—If the advance payments to a taxpayer under paragraph (2) for a calendar quarter exceed the credit allowed by this section (determined without regard to subparagraph (A)), the tax imposed by chapter 21 or 22 of the Internal Revenue Code of 1986 (whichever is applicable) for the calendar quarter shall be increased by the amount of such excess." .

(2) CONFORMING AMENDMENTS.— Section 2301(l) of the CARES Act, as amended by section 206 and subsection (d)(2)(B), is amended—

(A) by inserting "as provided in subsection (j)(2)" after "subsection (a)" in paragraph (1),

(B) by striking paragraph (2), and

(C) by redesignating paragraphs (3) and (4) as paragraphs (2) and (3), respectively.

(h) THIRD-PARTY PAYORS.— Section 2301(l) of the CARES Act, as amended by section 206 and subsections (d)(2)(B) and (g)(2), is amended by adding at the end the following flush sentence:

"Any forms, instructions, regulations, or guidance described in paragraph (2) shall require the customer to be responsible for the accounting of the credit and for any liability for improperly claimed credits and shall require the certified professional employer organization or other third party payor to accurately report such tax credits based on the information provided by the customer." .

(i) PUBLIC AWARENESS CAMPAIGN.— Section 2301 of the CARES Act is amended by adding at the end the following new subsection:

"(n) PUBLIC AWARENESS CAMPAIGN.—

"(1) IN GENERAL.—The Secretary shall conduct a public awareness campaign, in coordination with the Administrator of the Small Business Administration, to provide information regarding the availability of the credit allowed under this section.

"(2) OUTREACH.—Under the campaign conducted under paragraph (1), the Secretary shall—

"(A) provide to all employers which reported not more than 500 employees on the most recently filed return of applicable employment taxes a notice about the credit allowed under this section and the requirements for eligibility to claim the credit, and

"(B) not later than 30 days after the date of the enactment of this subsection, provide to all employers educational materials relating to the credit allowed under this section, including specific materials for businesses with not more than 500 employees." .

(j) COORDINATION WITH CERTAIN PAYROLL PROTECTION PROGRAM LOANS.— Section 2301(g)(2) of the CARES Act, as added by section 206(c)(2)(A), is amended by striking "section 7A(g) of the Small Business Act" and all that follows and inserting "section 7A(g) of the Small Business Act or the application of section 7(a)(37)(J) of the Small Business Act. Terms used in the preceding sentence which are also used in section 7A(g) or 7(a)(37)(J) of the Small Business Act shall, when applied in connection with either such section, have the same meaning as when used in such section, respectively." .

(k) EFFECTIVE DATE.— The amendments made by this section shall apply to calendar quarters beginning after December 31, 2020.

SEC. 303. EMPLOYEE RETENTION CREDIT FOR EMPLOYERS AFFECTED BY QUALIFIED DISASTERS. —

(a) IN GENERAL.— For purposes of section 38 of the Internal Revenue Codeof 1986, in the case of an eligible employer, the 2020 qualified disaster employee retention credit shall be treated as a credit listed at the end of subsection (b) of such section. For purposes of this subsection, the 2020 qualified disaster employee retention credit for any taxable year is an amount equal to 40 percent of the qualified wages with respect to each eligible employee of such employer for such taxable year. The amount of qualified wages with respect to any employee which may be taken into account under this subsection by the employer for any taxable year shall not exceed $6,000 (reduced by the amount of qualified wages with respect to such employee taken into account for any prior taxable year).

(b) DEFINITIONS.— For purposes of this section—

(1) ELIGIBLE EMPLOYER.— The term "eligible employer" means any employer—

(A) which conducted an active trade or business in a qualified disaster zone at any time during the incident period of the qualified disaster with respect to such qualified disaster zone, and

(B) with respect to whom the trade or business described in subparagraph (A) is inoperable at any time during the period beginning on the first day of the incident period of such qualified disaster and ending on the date of the enactment of this Act, as a result of damage sustained by reason of such qualified disaster.

(2) ELIGIBLE EMPLOYEE.— The term "eligible employee" means with respect to an eligible employer an employee whose principal place of employment with such eligible employer (determined immediately before the qualified disaster referred to in paragraph (1)) was in the qualified disaster zone referred to in such paragraph.

(3) QUALIFIED WAGES.— The term "qualified wages" means wages (as defined in section 51(c)(1) of the Internal Revenue Code of 1986, but without regard to section 3306(b)(2)(B) of such Code) paid or incurred by an eligible employer with respect to an eligible employee at any time on or after the date on which the trade or business described in paragraph (1) first became inoperable at the principal place of employment of the employee (determined immediately before the qualified disaster referred to in such paragraph) and before the earlier of—

(A) the date on which such trade or business has resumed significant operations at such principal place of employment, or

(B) the date which is 150 days after the last day of the incident period of the qualified disaster referred to in paragraph (1).

Such term shall include wages paid without regard to whether the employee performs no services, performs services at a different place of employment than such principal place of employment, or performs services at such principal place of employment before significant operations have resumed. Such term shall not include any wages taken into account under section 2301 of the CARES Act.

(c) SPECIAL RULES.—

(1) DENIAL OF DOUBLE BENEFIT.— Any wages taken into account in determining any credit allowed under this section shall not be taken into account as wages for purposes of sections 41, 45A, 45P, 45S, 51, and 1396 of the Internal Revenue Code of 1986.

(2) CERTAIN OTHER RULES TO APPLY.— For purposes of this section, rules similar to the rules of sections 51(i)(1), 52, and 280C(a) of the Internal Revenue Code of 1986 shall apply.

(d) PAYROLL TAX CREDIT FOR CERTAIN TAX-EXEMPT ORGANIZATIONS.—

(1) IN GENERAL.— In the case of any qualified tax-exempt organization, there shall be allowed as a credit against the tax imposed by section 3111(a) of the Internal Revenue Code of 1986 on wages paid with respect to employment of all employees of the organization during the calendar quarter an amount equal to 40 percent of the qualified wages paid to eligible employees of such organization during such calendar quarter.

(2) APPLICATION OF AGGREGATE DOLLAR LIMITATION PER EMPLOYEE.— The amount of qualified wages with respect to any employee which may be taken into account under this subsection by the employer for any calendar quarter shall not exceed $6,000 (reduced by the amount of qualified wages with respect to which credit was allowed under this subsection for any prior calendar quarter with respect to such employee).

(3) OVERALL LIMITATION.—

(A) IN GENERAL.— The aggregate amount allowed as a credit under this subsection for all eligible employees of any employer for any calendar quarter shall not exceed the amount of the tax imposed by section 3111(a) of the Internal Revenue Code of 1986 on wages paid with respect to employment of all employees of such employer during such calendar quarter (reduced by any credits allowed under subsections (e) and (f) of section 3111 of such Code for such quarter).

(B) CARRYFORWARD.— If the amount of the credit under paragraph (1) exceeds the limitation of subparagraph (A) for any calendar quarter, such excess shall be carried to the succeeding calendar quarter and allowed as a credit under paragraph (1) for such quarter.

(C) COORDINATION WITH OTHER PAYROLL TAX CREDITS.—

(i) Section 7001(b)(3) of the Families First Coronavirus Response Act is amended by inserting ", and section 303(d) of the Taxpayer Certainty and Disaster Tax Relief Act of 2020," after "subsections (e) and (f) of section 3111 of such Code".

(ii) Section 7003(b)(2) of the Families First Coronavirus Response Act is amended by striking "and section 7001 of this Act," and inserting "section 7001 of this Act, and section 303(d) of the Taxpayer Certainty and Disaster Tax Relief Act of 2020,".

(iii) Section 2301(b)(2) of the CARES Act is amended by striking "and sections 7001 and 7003 of the Families First Coronavirus Response Act" and inserting ", sections 7001 and 7003 of the Families First Coronavirus Response Act, and section 303(d) of the Taxpayer Certainty and Disaster Tax Relief Act of 2020".

(4) DEFINITIONS.—

(A) QUALIFIED TAX-EXEMPT ORGANIZATION.— For purposes of this subsection, the term "qualified tax-exempt organization" means an organization described in section 501(c) of the Internal Revenue Code of 1986 and exempt from taxation under section 501(a) of such Code if such organization would be an eligible employer if the activities of such organization were an active trade or business.

(B) APPLICATION OF CERTAIN TERMS WITH RESPECT TO QUALIFIED TAX-EXEMPT ORGANIZATIONS.— For purposes of this subsection, the terms "eligible employee" and "qualified wages" shall be applied with respect to any qualified tax-exempt organization—

(i) by treating the activities of such organization as an active trade or business, and

(ii) by substituting "wages (within the meaning of subsection (d)(4)(C))" for "wages (as defined in section 51(c)(1) of the Internal Revenue Code of 1986, but without regard to section 3306(b)(2)(B) of such Code)" in subsection (b)(3).

(C) OTHER TERMS.— Except as otherwise provided in this subsection, any term used in this subsection which is also used in chapter 21 or 22 of the Internal Revenue Code of 1986 shall have the same meaning as when used in such chapter.

(5) TRANSFERS TO CERTAIN TRUST FUNDS.— There are hereby appropriated to the Federal Old-Age and Survivors Insurance Trust Fund and the Federal Disability Insurance Trust Fund established under section 201 of the Social Security Act (42 U.S.C. 401) and the Social Security Equivalent Benefit Account established under section 15A(a) of the Railroad Retirement Act of 1974 (45 U.S.C. 231n-1(a)) amounts equal to the reduction in revenues to the Treasury by reason of this subsection (without regard to this paragraph). Amounts appropriated by the preceding sentence shall be transferred from the general fund at such times and in such manner as to replicate to the extent possible the transfers which would have occurred to such Trust Fund or Account had this subsection not been enacted.

(6) TREATMENT OF DEPOSITS.— The Secretary shall waive any penalty under section 6656 of such Code for any failure to make a deposit of applicable employment taxes if the Secretary determines that such failure was due to the anticipation of the credit allowed under this subsection.

(7) THIRD PARTY PAYORS.— Any credit allowed under this subsection shall be treated as a credit described in section 3511(d)(2) of such Code.

(8) COORDINATION WITH SUBSECTION (a) CREDIT.— Any wages taken into account in determining the credit allowed under this subsection shall not be take into account as wages for purposes of subsection (a).

(9) REGULATIONS AND GUIDANCE.— The Secretary shall issue such forms, instructions, regulations, and guidance as are necessary—

>(A) to allow the advance payment of the credit under paragraph (1), subject to the limitations provided in this subsection, based on such information as the Secretary shall require,
>
>(B) regulations or other guidance to provide for the reconciliation of such advance payment with the amount of the credit under this subsection at the time of filing the return of tax for the applicable quarter or taxable year,
>
>(C) with respect to the application of the credit under paragraph (1) to third party payors (including professional employer organizations, certified professional employer organizations, or agents under section 3504 of the Internal Revenue Code of 1986), including regulations or guidance allowing such payors to submit documentation necessary to substantiate the eligible employer status of employers that use such payors, and
>
>(D) for recapturing the benefit of credits determined under this subsection in cases where there is a subsequent adjustment to the credit determined under paragraph (1).

(e) ELECTION TO NOT TAKE CERTAIN WAGES INTO ACCOUNT.—

(1) IN GENERAL.— This section shall not apply to qualified wages paid by an eligible employer with respect to which such employer makes an election (at such time and in such manner as the Secretary may prescribe) to have this section not apply to such wages.

(2) COORDINATION WITH PAYCHECK PROTECTION PROGRAM.— The Secretary, in consultation with the Administrator of the Small Business Administration, shall issue guidance providing that payroll costs paid or incurred during the covered period shall not fail to be treated as qualified wages under this section by reason of an election under paragraph (1) to the extent that a covered loan of the eligible employer is not forgiven by reason of a decision under section 7A(g) of the Small Business Act. Terms used in the preceding sentence which are also used in section 7A(g) of such Act shall have the same meaning as when used in such section.

(f) CERTAIN GOVERNMENTAL EMPLOYERS.—

(1) IN GENERAL.— The credits under this section shall not apply to the Government of the United States, the government of any State or political subdivision thereof, or any agency or instrumentality of any of the foregoing.

(2) EXCEPTION.— Paragraph (1) shall not apply to—

(A) any organization described in section 501(c)(1) of the Internal Revenue Code of 1986 and exempt from tax under section 501(a) of such Code, or

(B) any entity described in paragraph (1) if —

(i) such entity is a college or university, or

(ii) the principal purpose or function of such entity is providing medical or hospital care.

An entity described in subparagraph (B) shall be treated for purposes of this section in the same manner as an organization described in section 501(c) of the Internal Revenue Code of 1986 and exempt from tax under section 501(a) of such Code.

(g) AMENDMENT TO PAYCHECK PROTECTION PROGRAM.— Section 7A(a)(12) of the Small Business Act (as redesignated, transferred, and amended by the Economic Aid to Hard-Hit Small Businesses, Nonprofits, and Venues Act and as amended by section 206(c) of this division) is amended by adding at the end the following: "Such payroll costs shall not include qualified wages taken into account in determining the credit allowed under subsection (a) or (d) of section 303 of the Taxpayer Certainty and Disaster Tax Relief Act of 2020.".

Appendix C: Section 3134

American Rescue Plan Act of 2021, Public Law 2, 117th Cong., 1st sess. (March 11, 2021), sec. 3134

SEC. 9651. EXTENSION OF EMPLOYEE RETENTION CREDIT.

(a) IN GENERAL.—Subchapter D of chapter 21 of subtitle C of the Internal Revenue Code of 1986, as added by section 9641, is amended by adding at the end the following:

"SEC. 3134. EMPLOYEE RETENTION CREDIT FOR EMPLOYERS SUBJECT TO CLOSURE DUE TO COVID-19.

"(a) IN GENERAL.—In the case of an eligible employer, there shall be allowed as a credit against applicable employment taxes for each calendar quarter an amount equal to 70 percent of the qualified wages with respect to each employee of such employer for such calendar quarter.

"(b) LIMITATIONS AND REFUNDABILITY.—

"(1) IN GENERAL.—

"(A) WAGES TAKEN INTO ACCOUNT.—The amount of qualified wages with respect to any employee which may be taken into account under subsection (a) by the eligible employer for any calendar quarter shall not exceed $10,000.

"(B) RECOVERY STARTUP BUSINESSES.—In the case of an eligible employer which is a recovery startup business (as defined in subsection (c)(5)), the amount of the credit allowed under subsection (a) (after application of subparagraph (A)) for any calendar quarter shall not exceed $50,000.

"(2) CREDIT LIMITED TO EMPLOYMENT TAXES.—The credit allowed by subsection (a) with respect to any calendar quarter shall not exceed the applicable employment taxes (reduced by any credits allowed under sections 3131 and 3132) on the wages paid with respect to the employment of all the employees of the eligible employer for such calendar quarter.

"(3) REFUNDABILITY OF EXCESS CREDIT.—If the amount of the credit under subsection (a) exceeds the limitation of paragraph (2) for any calendar quarter, such excess shall be treated as an overpayment that shall be refunded under sections 6402(a) and 6413(b).

"(c) DEFINITIONS.—For purposes of this section—

"(1) APPLICABLE EMPLOYMENT TAXES.—The term 'applicable employment taxes' means the following:

"(A) The taxes imposed under section 3111(b).

"(B) So much of the taxes imposed under section 3221(a) as are attributable to the rate in effect under section 3111(b).

"(2) ELIGIBLE EMPLOYER.—

"(A) IN GENERAL.—The term 'eligible employer' means any employer—

"(i) which was carrying on a trade or business during the calendar quarter for which the credit is determined under subsection (a), and

"(ii) with respect to any calendar quarter, for which—

"(I) the operation of the trade or business described in clause (i) is fully or partially suspended during the calendar quarter due to orders from an appropriate governmental authority limiting commerce, travel, or group meetings (for commercial, social, religious, or other purposes) due to the coronavirus disease 2019 (COVID–19),

"(II) the gross receipts (within the meaning of section 448(c)) of such employer for such calendar quarter are less than 80 percent of the gross receipts of such employer for the same calendar quarter in calendar year 2019, or

"(III) the employer is a recovery startup business (as defined in paragraph (5)).

With respect to any employer for any calendar quarter, if such employer was not in existence as of the beginning of the same calendar quarter in calendar year 2019, clause (ii)(II) shall be applied by substituting '2020' for '2019'.

"(B) ELECTION TO USE ALTERNATIVE QUARTER.—At the election of the employer—

"(i) subparagraph (A)(ii)(II) shall be applied—

"(I) by substituting 'for the immediately preceding calendar quarter' for 'for such calendar quarter', and

"(II) by substituting 'the corresponding calendar quarter in calendar year 2019' for 'the same calendar quarter in calendar year 2019', and

"(ii) the last sentence of subparagraph (A) shall be applied by substituting 'the corresponding calendar quarter in calendar year 2019' for 'the same calendar quarter in calendar year 2019'.

An election under this subparagraph shall be made at such time and in such manner as the Secretary shall prescribe.

"(C) TAX-EXEMPT ORGANIZATIONS.— In the case of an organization which is described in section 501(c) and exempt from tax under section 501(a)—

"(i) clauses (i) and (ii)(I) of subparagraph (A) shall apply to all operations of such organization, and

"(ii) any reference in this section to gross receipts shall be treated as a reference to gross receipts within the meaning of section 6033.

"(3) QUALIFIED WAGES.—

"(A) IN GENERAL.— The term 'qualified wages' means—

"(i) in the case of an eligible employer for which the average number of full-time employees (within the meaning of section 4980H) employed by such eligible employer during 2019 was greater than 500, wages paid by such eligible employer with respect to which an employee is not providing services due to circumstances described in subclause (I) or (II) of paragraph (2)(A)(ii), or "(ii) in the case of an eligible employer for which the average number of full-time employees (within the meaning of section 4980H) employed by such eligible employer during 2019 was not greater than 500 —

"(I) with respect to an eligible employer described in subclause (I) of paragraph (2)(A)(ii), wages paid by such eligible employer with respect to an employee during any period described in such clause, or

"(II) with respect to an eligible employer described in subclause (II) of such paragraph, wages paid by such eligible employer with respect to an employee during such quarter.

"(B) SPECIAL RULE FOR EMPLOYERS NOT IN EXISTENCE IN 2019. — In the case of any employer that was not in existence in 2019, subparagraph (A) shall be applied by substituting '2020' for '2019' each place it appears.

"(C) SEVERELY FINANCIALLY DISTRESSED EMPLOYERS. —

"(i) IN GENERAL. — Notwithstanding subparagraph (A)(i), in the case of a severely financially distressed employer, the term 'qualified wages' means wages paid by such employer with respect to an employee during any calendar quarter.

"(ii) DEFINITION. — The term 'severely financially distressed employer' means an eligible employer as defined in paragraph (2), determined by substituting 'less than 10 percent' for 'less than 80 percent' in subparagraph (A)(ii)(II) thereof.

"(D) EXCEPTION.—The term 'qualified wages' shall not include any wages taken into account under sections 41, 45A, 45P, 45S, 51, 1396, 3131, and 3132.

"(4) WAGES.—

"(A) IN GENERAL.—The term 'wages' means wages (as defined in section 3121(a)) and compensation (as defined in section 3231(e)). For purposes of the preceding sentence, in the case of any organization or entity described in subsection (f)(2), wages as defined in section 3121(a) shall be determined without regard to paragraphs (5), (6), (7), (10), and (13) of section 3121(b) (except with respect to services performed in a penal institution by an inmate thereof).

"(B) ALLOWANCE FOR CERTAIN HEALTH PLAN EXPENSES.—

"(i) IN GENERAL.—Such term shall include amounts paid by the eligible employer to provide and maintain a group health plan (as defined in section 5000(b)(1)), but only to the extent that such amounts are excluded from the gross income of employees by reason of section 106(a).

"(ii) ALLOCATION RULES.—For purposes of this section, amounts treated as wages under clause (i) shall be treated as paid with respect to any employee (and with respect to any period) to the extent that such amounts are properly allocable to such employee (and to such period) in such manner as the Secretary may prescribe. Except as otherwise provided by the Secretary, such allocation shall be treated as properly made if made on the basis of being pro rata among periods of coverage.

"(5) RECOVERY STARTUP BUSINESS.—The term 'recovery startup business' means any employer—

"(A) which began carrying on any trade or business after February 15, 2020,

"(B) for which the average annual gross receipts of such employer (as determined under rules similar to the rules under section 448(c)(3)) for the 3-taxable-year period ending with the taxable year which precedes the calendar quarter for which the credit is determined under subsection (a) does not exceed $1,000,000, and

"(C) which, with respect to such calendar quarter, is not described in subclause (I) or (II) of paragraph (2)(A)(ii).

"(6) OTHER TERMS.—Any term used in this section which is also used in this chapter or chapter 22 shall have the same meaning as when used in such chapter.

"(d) AGGREGATION RULE.—All persons treated as a single employer under subsection (a) or (b) of section 52, or subsection (m) or (o) of section 414, shall be treated as one employer for purposes of this section.

"(e) CERTAIN RULES TO APPLY.—For purposes of this section, rules similar to the rules of sections 51(i)(1) and 280C(a) shall apply.

"(f) CERTAIN GOVERNMENTAL EMPLOYERS.—

"(1) IN GENERAL.—This credit shall not apply to the Government of the United States, the government of any State or political subdivision thereof, or any agency or instrumentality of any of the foregoing.

"(2) EXCEPTION.—Paragraph (1) shall not apply to—

"(A) any organization described in section 501(c)(1) and exempt from tax under section 501(a), or

"(B) any entity described in paragraph (1) if—

"(i) such entity is a college or university, or

"(ii) the principal purpose or function of such entity is providing medical or hospital care.

In the case of any entity described in subparagraph (B), such entity shall be treated as satisfying the requirements of subsection (c)(2)(A)(i).

"(g) ELECTION TO NOT TAKE CERTAIN WAGES INTO ACCOUNT.—This section shall not apply to so much of the qualified wages paid by an eligible employer as such employer elects (at such time and in such manner as the Secretary may prescribe) to not take into account for purposes of this section.

"(h) COORDINATION WITH CERTAIN PROGRAMS.—

"(1) IN GENERAL.—This section shall not apply to so much of the qualified wages paid by an eligible employer as are taken into account as payroll costs in connection with—

"(A) a covered loan under section 7(a)(37) or 7A of the Small Business Act,

"(B) a grant under section 324 of the Economic Aid to Hard-Hit Small Businesses, Non-Profits, and Venues Act, or

"(C) a restaurant revitalization grant under section 5003 of the American Rescue Plan Act of 2021.

"(2) APPLICATION WHERE PPP LOANS NOT FORGIVEN.—The Secretary shall issue guidance providing that payroll costs paid during the covered period shall not fail to be treated as qualified wages under this section by reason of paragraph (1) to the extent that—

"(A) a covered loan of the taxpayer under section 7(a)(37) of the Small Business Act is not forgiven by reason of a decision under section 7(a)(37)(J) of such Act, or

"(B) a covered loan of the taxpayer under section 7A of the Small Business Act is not forgiven by reason of a decision under section 7A(g) of such Act.

Terms used in the preceding sentence which are also used in section 7A(g) or 7(a)(37)(J) of the Small Business Act shall, when applied in connection with either such section, have the same meaning as when used in such section, respectively.

"(i) THIRD PARTY PAYORS.—Any credit allowed under this section shall be treated as a credit described in section 3511(d)(2).

"(j) ADVANCE PAYMENTS.—

"(1) IN GENERAL.—Except as provided in paragraph (2), no advance payment of the credit under subsection (a) shall be allowed.

"(2) ADVANCE PAYMENTS TO SMALL EMPLOYERS.—

"(A) IN GENERAL.—Under rules provided by the Secretary, an eligible employer for which the average number of full-time employees (within the meaning of section 4980H) employed by such eligible employer during 2019 was not greater than 500 may elect for any calendar quarter to receive an advance payment of the credit under subsection (a) for such quarter in an amount not to exceed 70 percent of the average quarterly wages paid by the employer in calendar year 2019.

"(B) SPECIAL RULE FOR SEASONAL EMPLOYERS.—In the case of any employer who employs seasonal workers (as defined in section 45R(d)(5)(B)), the employer may elect to apply subparagraph (A) by substituting 'the wages for the calendar quarter in 2019 which corresponds to the calendar quarter to which the election relates' for 'the average quarterly wages paid by the employer in calendar year 2019'.

"(C) SPECIAL RULE FOR EMPLOYERS NOT IN EXISTENCE IN 2019.—In the case of any employer that was not in existence in 2019, subparagraphs (A) and (B) shall each be applied by substituting '2020' for '2019' each place it appears.

"(3) RECONCILIATION OF CREDIT WITH ADVANCE PAYMENTS.—

"(A) IN GENERAL.—The amount of credit which would (but for this subsection) be allowed under this section shall be reduced (but not below zero) by the aggregate payment allowed to the taxpayer under paragraph (2). Any failure to so reduce the credit shall be treated as arising out of a mathematical or clerical error and assessed according to section 6213(b)(1).

"(B) EXCESS ADVANCE PAYMENTS.—If the advance payments to a taxpayer under paragraph (2) for a calendar quarter exceed the credit allowed by this section (determined without regard to subparagraph (A)), the tax imposed under section 3111(b) or so much of the tax imposed under section 3221(a) as is attributable to the rate in effect under section 3111(b) (whichever is applicable) for the calendar quarter shall be increased by the amount of such excess.

"(k) TREATMENT OF DEPOSITS.—The Secretary shall waive any penalty under section 6656 for any failure to make a deposit of any applicable employment taxes if the Secretary determines that such failure was due to the reasonable anticipation of the credit allowed under this section.

"(l) EXTENSION OF LIMITATION ON ASSESSMENT.—Notwithstanding section 6501, the limitation on the time period for the assessment of any amount attributable to a credit claimed under this section shall not expire before the date that is 5 years after the later of—

"(1) the date on which the original return which includes the calendar quarter with respect to which such credit is determined is filed, or

"(2) the date on which such return is treated as filed under section 6501(b)(2).

"(m) REGULATIONS AND GUIDANCE.— The Secretary shall issue such forms, instructions, regulations, and other guidance as are necessary—

"(1) to allow the advance payment of the credit under subsection (a) as provided in subsection (j)(2), subject to the limitations provided in this section, based on such information as the Secretary shall require,

"(2) with respect to the application of the credit under subsection (a) to third party payors (including professional employer organizations, certified professional employer organizations, or agents under section 3504), including regulations or guidance allowing such payors to submit documentation necessary to substantiate the eligible employer status of employers that use such payors, and

"(3) to prevent the avoidance of the purposes of the limitations under this section, including through the leaseback of employees.

Any forms, instructions, regulations, or other guidance described in paragraph (2) shall require the customer to be responsible for the accounting of the credit and for any liability for improperly claimed credits and shall require the certified professional employer organization or other third party payor to accurately report such tax credits based on the information provided by the customer.

"(n) APPLICATION.—This section shall only apply to wages paid after June 30, 2021, and before January 1, 2022.".

(b) REFUNDS.—Paragraph (2) of section 1324(b) of title 31, United States Code, is amended by inserting "3134," before "6428".

(c) CLERICAL AMENDMENT.—The table of sections for subchapter D of chapter 21 of subtitle C of the Internal Revenue Code of 1986 is amended by adding at the end the following:

"Sec. 3134. Employee retention credit for employers subject to closure due to COVID–19.".

(d) EFFECTIVE DATE.—The amendments made by this section shall apply to calendar quarters beginning after June 30, 2021.

www.ingramcontent.com/pod-product-compliance
Lightning Source LLC
Chambersburg PA
CBHW071500220526
45472CB00003B/863